How to Write Your Own Will

John C. Howell

© John C. Howell, 1985
LIBERTY PUBLISHING COMPANY
Cockeysville, Maryland

Published by:
Liberty Publishing Company, Inc.
50 Scott Adam Road
Cockeysville, Maryland 21030

This publication is designed to provide accurate and authoritative information in regard to the subject matter covered. It is sold with the understanding
that the publisher is not engaged in rendering legal, accounting or other
professional service. If legal advice or other expert assistance is required,
the services of a competent professional person should be sought.

—From a Declaration of Principles jointly
adopted by a Committee of the American Bar
Association and a Committee of Publishers.

Library of Congress #84-80942
ISBN 0-89709-137-X

Cover photo courtesy of
photographer Susan H. Cleveland.
Text edited by Arthur F. Ballant, Jr.

Manufactured USA

*Be wise today;
'tis madness to defer.*

Edward Young (1683-1765)

Contents

Preface

A few years ago, after 21 years of active law practice, I wrote my first book in a series of legal guides for the layman. This series, called The Citizens Law Library, was the beginning of my advocacy of the concept that the layman can handle many legal problems alone without a lawyer.

Shortly thereafter, the American Bar Association sponsored Assembly on Death, Taxes and Family Property reported that:

"The Bar should encourage the trend toward various devices permitting settlement of estates with little or no court involvement of lawyers. The development of procedures for transferring property without administration should be encouraged, as should 'do-it-yourself techniques.'" (63 ABA Journal 88, January 1977.)

The State of California, for example, authorized a statutory will for its citizens. The Do-It-Yourself concept is an idea whose time has come!

While many areas of the law lend themselves to do-it-yourself methods, several recent events have catapulted "writing your own will" and "avoiding probate" to the top of the list. Both are extremely easy to do yourself without an attorney. Moreover, recent changes in the Tax Code make these techniques irresistible do-it-yourself projects.

Needless to say, lawyers would like to discourage the practice of laymen solving their own legal problems. Many attorneys are still too egotistical to accept the basic concept that a layman can fill in the blanks of a form as easily as the attorney's secretary. Of course lawyers also object to losing legal fees. A will is now so easy to write it almost seems unreasonable to charge such high legal fees for such a simple service.

The Chief Justice of the United States, Warren Burger, once declared:

". . . ours is a sick profession," marked by "incompetence, lack of training, misconduct and bad manners. Ineptness, bungling, malpractice, and bad ethics can be observed in court houses all over this country every day." He added that these incompetents have "a seeming unawareness of the fundamental ethics of the profession."

Even other lawyers will admit that the bulk of what most lawyers do can be done by someone who has never seen the inside of a law school. Legal secretaries do most of the work on wills, divorces, annulments, legal separations, bankruptcies and creditor plans, simple contracts, real estate deals, and so on. The list goes on and on. The secretaries just follow the directions and fill in the blanks. It's really as simple as that!

Just a few years ago the idea of writing a will conjured up complex and technical problems such as estate taxes, marital deduction formulas and other details that seemingly required a lawyer. Now that has all changed.

First, the new tax code has raised the federal estate tax exemption so that more than 99% of all estates today are totally exempt from such taxes.

Secondly, the do-it-yourself concept — especially in will writing and avoiding probate — has been accepted by bar associations, lawyers, judges, legislative authorities, and the general public.

Under the new tax code, federal estate taxes generally do not become a problem until the taxable estate exceeds the new exempt amounts. For those decedents who died in 1984, the amount was $325,000, increasing to $400,000 in 1985, $500,000 in 1986, and $600,000 in 1987 and thereafter.

In addition to these basic exempt amounts, an unlimited amount can be transferred to a spouse, before or after death, without any estate or gift taxes. This means that very few estates will have any tax problems. It is estimated that less than 1% of the estates will be taxable. Thus, almost every American will now be able to write his or her own will without fear of any tax complications.

Without a will, your property would be distributed according to your state's Statute of Intestate Succession and Distribution, and you would have nothing to say about it! The probate court would be the one to decide on questions you didn't bother to answer. The court would appoint an administrator for your property and a guardian for your children. In other words, without a will, the whole probate process becomes more expensive, time consuming and inefficient.

If you can transfer some or all of your assets to another member of your family in a few hours or a few days at most, why does it take the probate court two, three or even five or more years to do the same thing after death? This is a question that lawyers would rather not answer. Probate lawyers, as a matter of routine, like to take their fee (perhaps 3% to 20% or more) from every estate they handle. Probate can be avoided, as explained fully in Part II of this book.

Today executors' and attorneys' fees total more than 1.5 billion dollars annually, which is equal to at least $12,000 (about 7%) of each estate. This percentage charge is, of course, generally higher for smaller estates and lower for those that are larger.

With this book, you can complete your own will in the privacy of your home without a lawyer, without intimidation, and without excessive legal fees. And it is all completely legal. The instructions and documents discussed herein are in accordance with the statutes of all 50 states. If you are an average American, this guide could be the only tool you'll ever need.

John C. Howell

Part I

How To Write Your Own Will

Introduction

Estate planning is the process of planning the creation, accumulation, conservation and utilization of estate resources to secure the maximum benefit now, during life, during disability, during retirement and after death.

Your will is one of the more important parts of a good estate plan, second in importance only to avoiding probate. All property owned by a decedent must be transferred to others in a legal way either by gift, will, by operation of law, living trust, private annuity or other probate and estate planning methods, or by a combination of these techniques.

You can write your own legal will without a lawyer, in the privacy of your own home. You will need complete information and instructions about the will writing process, the essential elements of a will, the laws governing wills, and the necessary forms for use in writing a will. This book is designed to provide all of the information and help you need to accomplish most of your estate planning objectives.

Now that over 99% of us are exempted from federal estate taxes, the standard basic will is all that most of us need. However, in addition to the basic will forms, there are a number of other forms in the event you feel a need for them.

You can use this information for all adult members of your family. If you can get over the inhibitions of talking about estate planning, this can be an interesting and worthwhile family project. Estate planning is an extremely important subject to all members of your family. Your will is effective only for transfer of those assets in your estate at the time of death. Assets transferred outside of the probate system by joint ownership, living trusts, gifts, private annuities or other probate avoidance techniques would not be affected by your will.

One of the great advantages of using this book is that you can change your estate plans at any time you have a need for change—or if you simply change your mind. Many people like to have this flexibility in their estate planning. People frequently complain that they want to change their will or some other item in their estate plans, but object to going back to the lawyer's office. They feel so intimidated by the lawyers and are inhibited by the excessive legal fees charged, even for a brief conference.

The do-it-yourself concept is not only an idea whose time has come. Writing your own will is now as simple and easy as writing a letter.

What Is A Will?

Definitions

A will is an instrument executed by a competent person in the manner prescribed by statute, whereby he makes a disposition of his property to take effect on and after his death. A document, to be a will, must be a testamentary in character, and must be executed in accordance with the requirements of the applicable state statute. An instrument is testamentary in character where, from the language used, it is apparent that the writer intended to make a disposition of his property, or some part of it, to be effective at death. In the absence of testamentary intent (*animus testandi*), there is no will. It is, of course, essential that a testator know and understand the contents of his will. A disposition of property is not a necessary requirement of a will even though it is generally the main reason most people write a will. A person may make a will for the sole purpose of nominating an executor, or to appoint a guardian.

A will must be ambulatory, that is, subject to change, and revocable during the maker's lifetime. The Latin phrase, *ambulatoria voluntas*, a changeable will, denotes the power which a testator possesses of altering his will during his lifetime. The term "testament," in early common law days, referred only to a disposition of real property. In modern usage, the term "will" includes every kind of testamentary act taking effect from the mind of the testator and manifested by an instrument in writing executed and attested in accordance with the statutes. Any writing, however informal it may be, made with the intent to dispose of property at the death of the writer, if executed in accordance with the statutory requirements, may be a good testamentary disposition. A letter, post card, memo, informal notes on envelopes, and other informal writings may constitute a will if they have the essential elements of a will. And, it is not essential in all states to have a will witnessed if certain other requirements are met.

For example, a nuncupative will is one that is not in writing, and exists only when the testator declares his will orally before witnesses. A holographic will or "olographic" will, valid in 23 states, is one that is entirely written and signed (and in some states, dated) by the testator in his own handwriting.

A codicil is some addition to, qualification of, or change of, one's will. Bequest is a gift of personal property, while legacy is a gift of property under a will. Devise means a gift of real property by will. A devisor is the one who leaves real property, while the devisee is the one who inherits real property through a devise.

Acknowledgment is a formal declaration before an authorized official, by a person who executed an instrument, that it is his free act and deed. If the decedent leaves a will designating a personal representative, the proper title for that representative is *executor* or *executrix*. (Throughout the rest of this book, the male-gender term *executor* will be used for both executor and executrix.) Guardian is a person lawfully vested with the power, and charged with the duty, of taking care of a person and managing the property rights of another person, who, for some peculiarity of status, or defect of age, understanding, or self-control, is considered incapable of administering his own affairs.

Intestate is the status of one who dies <u>without</u> a will. A *testator* (male) or *testatrix* (female) is one who dies leaving a will. The words execution, subscribe and subscription simply mean signing an instrument, usually at the end of it. In some states it is an absolute statutory requirement that a will be signed at the end. Attestation consists in witnessing the execution of the will by the testator in order to see and take notes mentally that those things are done which the statute requires for the execution of a will, and that the signature of the testator exists as a fact. The primary purpose of requiring that a will be attested is to render available proof that there has been a compliance with the statutory requisites of the execution of a will, and that the instrument offered for probate is the exact paper which the alleged testator signed, and not a surreptitious will, fraudulently substituted. Publication of a will consists in the communication by the testator to the attesting witnesses at the time they attest the instrument of his intention that it shall take effect as his will.

The Nature of Wills

In order to determine whether or not an instrument is a will, your intentions while writing the will must be ascertained. If you intend to dispose of your estate, the instrument is generally considered testamentary in character. The testamentary character of an instrument is determined by the interpretation of, and from the construction of, the language you use when writing the instrument. If it is clear that your intention is to dispose of your property after your death, the document contains sufficient testamentary character to constitute a will. The courts, in the interpretation of a will, generally consider the instrument as a whole. What property you have and how you intend to dispose of it must be clearly stated in the will. This cannot be done for you after your demise. The intent refers to an intent to dispose of property, not an intent to make a will. In other words, unless there is an intention to dispose of property, there is no will.

Predicatory Words

Unfortunately many people state in wills that they "wish" or "hope" or "desire" that certain things will occur with respect to their property. These words, when used in a will merely to suggest that the property be disposed of in a certain way, are not generally legally binding. Words that do not clearly indicate an intent to specifically dispose of your property should not be used. It is critical to avoid such terminology altogether or at least state as clearly as possible in writing what your true intentions are. The use of unclear language is an open invitation to lawsuits.

It is also essential that you know the contents of your will. It is usually presumed that a person who signs a written instrument knows the contents thereof, but this can be questioned. Uncertainty regarding these issues can be avoided by following the check list presented later in this book. A will written in a language that you do not understand may still be effective if you know and understand the contents. In fact, a blind person may validly sign a will if he knows and understands the contents of that will and has an intent to dispose of property.

Contents of Wills

There is no magic formula for what should be in a will, but the usual items include the following:
- a statement identifying the testator,
- special instructions on payment of debts,
- burial instructions and other general matters,
- appointment of executor or executrix, trustee or guardian,
- general and special disposition of property,
- residuary clause, and
- execution and attestation.

Scandalous or derogatory matters should never be placed in a will as this is another open invitation to unnecessary litigation. If scandalous matter does appear in a will, the court will usually disregard it; it has no place and it serves no purpose whatsoever. A properly executed will, under most laws, must be admitted to probate when offered.

Uncertain Provisions of Wills

The language you use in a will should be easily understood. When in doubt, it is better to use your own choice of words rather than to try to make the will sound "legal." It is necessary for a will to have a definite subject, in terms of property, and a definite or ascertainable object, in terms of persons, in order for there to be a valid disposition of property. Most courts will make an effort to correctly determine and interpret from the will just what you want so that your intentions can be carried out. This, indeed, is a major objective of the laws governing wills. A will which makes no disposition of property, but gives the executor "full authority" to divide the estate is void. It simply is not a will as defined by law in terms of accomplishing your objectives. You cannot let someone else do it for you, but you can establish a trust, appoint a trustee and grant powers of appointment.

Alterations and Changes

Writing between the lines and using erasures in a will are not recommended; if changes are desirable, the will should be retyped. However, if changes are made in accordance with the formalities required by law, the will as changed and altered will probably be admitted to probate. Any changes made in the will after your death can form no part of the will, and are of no effect whatsoever. Any changes in a will made by someone other than the testator himself and without his knowledge or consent, or with a bad motive or intention to deceive, or by accident or mistake, will not be effective. You may change your will as often as you choose, but it must be done strictly in accordance with the mandatory requirements of law.

Fraud, Mistake, and Undue Influence

Fraud, mistake, or undue influence are reasons for contesting the probate of a will or setting aside the probate of a will. The terms *fraud* and *undue influence* are closely associated and are frequently used together in most situations involving the contest of a will. The words *fraud, duress,* and *undue influence* are frequently used interchangeably by most courts. Some merely adopt the use of one word or the other depending upon the facts of the case. Using a broad generalization, undue influence is a type of fraud, even though it may have taken place without an active, affirmative, false statement or evil, wicked, and corrupt motive. Some courts have stated that a fradulent intent or motive is essential to cause undue influence to the point of invalidating a will. Other courts have stated that any influence which might have persuaded you when you wrote the will does not necessarily have to be fraudulent in order to invalidate the will. This is another legal issue that has no easy answer. Undue influence may be fraudulently exerted, but it is not inseparably connected with fraud. On the other hand, fraud may constitute a ground for contesting the validity of a will independent of undue influence. In all events the courts frequently struggle with a precise definition of the terms, but when a decision is made, it is usually a judgment based upon all the facts and circumstances. The courts merely use the appropriate words, phrases, or terms to state the conclusion reached.

If it can be established by good evidence that your will was written in error, the will may be declared void. In the absence of a law to the contrary, the validity of a will is not affected by a mistake of law unless fraud or undue influence was forced upon you or the mistake involves a want of testamentary intent. An example is one where you might execute the wrong instrument. The word *mistake* is used here in the sense of describing a chain of events or circumstances around which you sign the will, but because of the chain of events you did not intend to execute a valid will. A will is usually not denied probate merely because you do not understand or appreciate the effect of language used, so long as you have an intent to make a will.

Some laws provide that a *mistake of fact* may nullify in part the operation of a will provided that such a mistake is the result of ignorance and not an error of judgment after investigation or willful failure to make a proper investigation when the truth could have been determined. As a general rule, the courts will not declare an entire will invalid because of a *mistake* as to one phrase or paragraph.

Sufficient undue influence that may invalidate a will is not easy to define. Undue influence refers to the means and methods used by a person for the purpose of affecting and overcoming another. Undue influence is that which substitutes the wishes of another for your own wishes. It has often been stated that undue influence is an *unlawful influence*. It appears, however, that nothing more is meant by the expression than that it is the influence which deprives you of your freedom to act as you wish. A will may be contested successfully because of undue influence even though none of the acts that caused the influence may result in a civil or criminal liability charge. Acts performed with a good motive may nevertheless constitute undue influence.

The legal issues generated by claims of fraud, mistakes, or undue influence are very difficult to resolve. A careful review of this book, an analysis of your estate, and a properly drafted will can avoid all of these potential problems. Extra effort in the preparation and execution of your will may avoid the necessity of having some member of your family presented with these difficult questions in the future.

What Is Meant by a Basic Will or a Simple Will?

As a general rule, a one or two page will is entirely adequate for most people, married or unmarried. The term *simple will* is broadly and generally used in legal circles to describe a will for any person who does not have significant estate tax problems or legal entanglements requiring special provisions. Under the new tax code estate taxes generally do not become a problem until the taxable estate exceeds $600,000, (the exempt amount after 1986) and, of course, there is an unlimited marital exemption. Lawyers are sometimes reluctant to refer to a client's will as simple because they don't want the client to think his estate is small, and may not want the client to get the impression that the client's will is easy to prepare. In this book, the term *basic will* is used to describe the great majority of wills for estates with no significant estate tax problems and no unusual legal entanglements. This covers the vast majority of Americans. Essentially, in the absence of major tax or legal problems, the purpose of a will is rather basic: one simply appoints a representative and makes a disposition of property.

The basic will avoids the inconvenience and uncertainty of intestacy—the status of dying without any will. At the same time, you can appoint your executor or guardian to handle the administration of the estate rather than having some probate judge appoint one. Moreover, you can minimize the expenses of administration by waiving bonds in appropriate circumstances. If you fail to appoint an executor or guardian, there will be legal fees incurred in the proceedings to have the probate court make appointments. In most cases, it also causes some delays. Most married persons, with or without children, generally wish to have the entire estate go to the surviving spouse. This may not happen if you do not have a will. The basic will also makes provision for appointment of a guardian for minor children in the event of simultaneous deaths or where a spouse is predeceased, and a provision for a trust for minors.

Thus, the basic will is all that is needed by most people. The basic will for an unmarried person is essentially the same as the basic will for married persons, with minor changes to delete certain provisions, such as common disaster clauses. Marital deduction clauses are no longer needed as there is now an unlimited marital exemption.

Special Kinds of Wills

While the primary purpose of this book is to enable you to understand the basic legal principles governing wills, enable you to draft your own will, and execute your will in accordance with the statutory requirements of your state, there are some special kinds of wills with which you should become familiar. These include the holographic (handwritten) will and the nuncupative (oral) will. There are also special wills under the Louisiana Civil Code, but these aren't discussed, since the holographic will may be the best method for residents of that state.

Holographic Wills

Some state statutes permit a person to write a valid holographic will in his own handwriting with no witnesses needed, while others do not. Some of the statutes require that the will be written, dated, and signed entirely in the testator's own handwriting. Other statutes, based on the Uniform Probate Code, require only that the signature and the material provisions of the will be in the testator's handwriting. By requiring only the material provisions to be in the testator's handwriting, such holographic wills may be valid even though immaterial parts such as the date or introductory wording be printed or stamped. Under these statutes a valid holographic will might even be executed on some printed will forms if the printed portion could be eliminated and the handwritten portion could evidence the testator's will. For some persons unable to obtain legal assistance, the holographic will is entirely adequate.

A holographic will is an unwitnessed, unattested will which is entirely in the testator's handwriting. The holographic will as a distinct type originated in French law. Express provision for it was made in the Code of Napoleon; and this provision, in substantially the same form, was carried over into the Louisiana Civil Code. According to Section 970 of the Code Napoleon,

"A holographic testament shall not be valid, unless it be written entirely, dated and signed by the testator with his own hand; it is subject to no other form."

The recognition given such an instrument as a valid testamentary instrument despite the lack of compliance with the formalities of attestation is attributed to the fact that a successful counterfeit of another's handwriting is exceedingly difficult and that the requirement that it be in the testator's handwriting would afford protection against forgery. Although written by the testator himself, a holographic will is a solemn act; and no matter how clearly it conveys the wishes of the decedent, if it does not meet the statutory requirements, it is not valid. It is sufficient if the writing expresses, however informally, a testamentary purpose in language sufficiently clear to be understood.

A Letter as a Holographic Will

Since a holographic will is one that is entirely written and signed by the testator in his own handwriting, a letter in the handwriting of the testator may qualify as a will although it is not witnessed if it has the necessary testamentary character. A simple letter is the most common type of instrument sought to be probated as a will or codicil. Many people prefer the holographic method of disposing of their property.

In authorizing letters testamentary in character to be admitted to probate, the courts have attached no particular significance to the type of letter involved. Even a postcard may be probated as a will or codicil provided it is testamentary in character and meets the requisites of a handwritten will. Even if a letter does not meet the formal requisites of a will or codicil in the state where it is sought to be probated, if it meets the requisites in the state where it was written, it may, under applicable statutes, be probated as a valid will.

In order to be a will, it is an absolute requirement that the document be signed by the testator. This does not always mean a legal or formal signature. Any form of signature, even though it is abbreviated, will be approved if it is possible to identify the signer as the person involved. If the document was signed with an intent to dispose of property, it is generally held to be a valid will.

Some state statutes require that a holographic will be dated, as well as signed and written, in the hand of the testator. Under statutes requiring a date, the year, month, and day must be given, according to most courts. The fact that the letter is dated incorrectly does not render it void.

A letter dictated by the writer and actually written by a third person, or typewritten, either by the decedent or by someone on his behalf, or printed, does not meet the requisites of a holographic will, and is governed by the ordinary rules applicable to formal wills. This means that such a document would require signing and witnessing as in the case of regular statutory wills.

Testamentary Character

In order for a document, such as a letter, to be a last will and testament, it must, in addition to meeting all other legal requirements, clearly show that the decedent intended it to take effect only after his death. It is also necessary that it appear from the document that the decedent intended, by the very paper itself, to make a disposition of his property after his death. Testamentary character of the document is not the testator's realization that it is a will, but his intention to create a revocable disposition of his property. Casual statements, suggestions, wishes, recommendations, or requests are not dispositive, and generally do not make a will.

By way of example, the following writings have been held by the courts to be of sufficient testamentary intent to make a valid holographic will.

- "This is to serifey that ie levet to mey wife Real and persnal and she to dispose for them as she wis ..." (dated and signed, is not vague and uncertain, and devises to the wife all the real and personal property of the husband). *Mitchell, et al., v. Donahue, 34 P 614 (Calif 1893).*
- "dear bill i want you to have farm Annie Kaufman." *In re Kaufman's Will, 365 Pa 555, 76 A 2d 414.*
- "Dear old Nance: I wish to give you my watch, two shawls, and also five thousand dollars. Your old friend, E. A. Gordon." *Clarke v. Ransom, 50 Cal 595.*
- "If I die or get killed in Texas, the place must belong to you, and I would not want you to sell it." *Alston v. Davis, 118 N.C. 202, 24 S.E. 15.*
-   "July 7, 1949

  "Dear Catherine:

  "Just a few lines to let you know I am starting to Monaco, and I was very pleased with the vacation. Catherine, I want you to know you are to get all I have when I die. Tell Mary Agnes and David that Uncle George said hello and give them a big hug and a kiss for me.

  "I remain as ever

          "Uncle George Thompson." *Appeal of James Thompson, 375 Pa 193, 100 A 2d 69, 40 A.L.R. 2d 694.*
- "... if enny thing happens all ... (money bonds, saving stamps and home) goes to George Darl & Irvin Kepp this letter lock it up it may help you out." *Re Kimmel's Estate, 278 Pa 435, 123 A 405.*

On the other hand, a statement in a letter that "After all is said and done I intend to leave you and Reba what I have some day," did not show testamentary intent. *Poff v. Kaufman, 276 S.W. 2d 432.*

Signature

The important factor in determining whether the signature on a letter offered as a will or codicil is sufficient though abbreviated or otherwise different from the formal signature of the writer is whether the word or words were affixed to the paper with the intent that they constitute a signature, and sufficiently show who signed the paper.

As a general rule, the courts have held that the signing of a descriptive title relating to relationships, such as mother, father, brother, or aunt, is valid as a signature to a holographic will if the testator or testatrix wrote with the intent to execute the will. The courts have generally held that initials are sufficient if signed with the intent to execute the holographic will.

For example, the following have been held as valid signatures:

- "Your loving mother."
- "Father" *Re Kimmel's Estate (1924) 278 Pa 435, 123 A 405.*
- "Pop" *Kling, Sr. Estate (1956) 12 Pa D & C 2d 588.*
- "Brother Alex" *Wise v. Short (1921) 181 N.C. 320, 197 S.E. 134.*
- "Ant Nanie" *Wells v. Lewis (1921) 190 Ky 626, 228 S.W. 3.*
- "Lus" *Cartwright v. Cartwright, (1923) 158 Ark 278, 250 S.W. 11.*

Date

A date has been held not essentiial to the validity of a holographic will unless it is expressly required by statute. Where the date is required by statute, as in some states, it must be dated by the testator in his own handwriting. The date adds verity to the instrument; if the instrument is a forgery the date may furnish the means of detecting the fraud. The date may also be important in some cases to determine the testamentary capacity of the testator. Moreover, if there are two or more wills it is essential to have dates to determine the priorities of the documents. In those states where a date is required the courts have been strict in requiring that the date be definite, complete, and certain. Usually the day, month, and year are required.

Holographic Wills Under the Uniform Probate Code

The Uniform Code recommends the authorization of holographic wills and suggests more liberal wording in the statutes. The recommended language of the Uniform Code for the holographic will statute as proposed by the commissioners is as follows:

Section 2-503.   Holographic Will.   A will which does not comply with Section 2-502 is valid as a holographic will, whether or not witnessed, if the signature and the material provisions are in the handwriting of the testator.

The comment by the commissioners on the holographic will statute is as follows:

This section enables a testator to write his own will in his handwriting. There need be no witnesses. The only requirement is that the signature and the material provisions of the will be in the testator's handwriting. By requiring only the *material provisions* to be in the testator's handwriting (rather than requiring, as some existing statutes do, that the will be *entirely* in the testator's handwriting) a holograph may be valid even though immaterial parts such as date or introductory wording be printed or stamped. A valid holograph might even be executed on some printed will forms if the printed portion could be eliminated and the handwriting portion could evidence the testator's will. For persons unable to obtain legal assistance, the holographic will may be adequate.

The statutes (numbers next to state names indicate the section of that state's statutes) of each of the 23 states where holographic wills are valid are summarized, paraphrased, or quoted to give you a good idea of the laws of each state.

- Holographic wills are valid where the signature and the material provisions of the will are made in the handwriting of the testator in the following states:

Alaska	13.11.160
Arizona	14-2503
Colorado	15-11-503
Idaho	15-2-503
Maine	18A-2-503
Michigan	27.5123
Montana	91A-2-503
Nebraska	30-2328
New Jersey	3B-3-3
North Dakota	30.1-08-03

Tennessee 32-105
Utah 75-2-503
Wyoming 2-6-113

- When the entire body of the will and the signature are in the handwriting of the testator, it may be established by the evidence of at least three distinterested witnesses to the handwriting and signature of the testator, without subscribing witnesses in:

Arkansas 60-404

- A will written entirely in the testator's handwriting and signed and dated by him is valid in the following states:

California ...... Probate Code 53
Louisiana .... C.C. 1588
Nevada 133.090
Oklahoma 84.54
South Dakota 29-2-8

- A holographic will is valid if it is wholly written and subscribed by the testator in the following states:

Mississippi 91-5-1
Virginia 64.1-49
West Virginia 41-1-3

- A will wholly written by the testator is valid in:

Texas .... Probate Code 60

For those who reside in these states the holographic will is entirely adequate, and they are easy to write.

Nuncupative Wills

A nuncupative will is one that is not in writing, and exists only when the testator declares his will orally before witnesses. At early common law, it was not essential to the validity of a nuncupative will that the testator be ill, and there were no restrictions on the time of making it. To guard against the frauds for which oral wills seemed to offer so many facilities, provision was made in the original statute of frauds in England that a nuncupative will to be valid must be *made in the time of the last sickness.* The privilege of leaving a nuncupative will, it was generally held at that time, was to be exercised as a matter of necessity, not of choice.

In American courts, the cases dealing with what constitute a *last sickness*, within the meaning of the requirement that a nuncupative will must be executed when the alleged testator is in that condition, fall roughly into two categories: those that follow the doctrine that, to be in his *last sickness* within the meaning of statutes relating to nuncupative wills, a putative testator must have been *in extremis*, and those which do not require an *in extremis* condition as a condition to showing the alleged testator was in his *last sickness*.

The rationale supporting the first category of cases is that a nuncupative will is not good unless it is made by a testator when he is *in extremis*, or overtaken by sudden and violent illness, and has not time or opportunity to make a written will. If nuncupative wills can be permitted at all in case of chronic disorders, according to the reasoning, it could be only in the very last stage and extremity of them. A full statement of the rule is that to be valid, a nuncupative will must have been made when the testator was *in extremis*, or overtaken by sudden and violent illness, when he had neither time nor opportunity to make a written will.

The second category of cases are based upon the conclusion that it is not necessary to label an alleged testator's condition as *in extremis* to find that he was in his *last sickness* when he attempted a nuncupation. Perhaps most of these rulings inferentially reflect what some of them expressly declare, namely, that the term last sickness simply means the sickness from which the deceased did not recover. Some courts have said that to require the testator to have been *in extremis* is adding words to the statute. It has also been reasoned that a too strict interpretation of the term *last sickness* might compel that stage of final illness so close to death that testamentary capacity would be lost.

These difficulties tend to support the suggestion made in the cases that one should not seriously rely upon nuncupative wills. A *gift causa mortis*, where one, in contemplation of death, delivers a gift to another person, may be more effective in many circumstances than a nuncupative will.

Who May Make A Will?

Your right to designate who will receive your property is dependent upon your possession of testamentary power and testamentary capacity. It is important to know and understand the distinction between testamentary capacity and testamentary power. Testamentary power is the right, by will, to pass property to others of your choosing; that is, what property may be willed and to whom it may be given. This right is granted by the state statutes. Before you can transfer property by will, it is necessary that you possess both testamentary capacity and testamentary power. Testamentary capacity relates to the competency to make a will. For the most part, if you have testamentary power and capacity, you may dispose of your property by will to such persons and for such purposes as you choose, provided, of course, that such disposition is not contrary to the law or public policy.

Testamentary Capacity

Any person of sound mind and disposing memory and of proper age may make a will disposing of real and personal property. This is called testamentary capacity and is regulated by state statutes. Variations in these statutory provisions covering testamentary age range from 14 years to 21 years.

The capacity to make a will is determined as of the time of the execution of the will. If capacity exists at the time you write your will, it should be valid. It does not matter that you may not have had the competency, or capacity, to write a will some years ago or that you may become incapacitated, or incompetent, sometime in the future. The important thing is that you had the capacity when the will was written. The issue of capacity or competency is a question of fact that will be determined by a court should a contest develop. It is this possibility, however, which makes it extremely important for you to carefully follow these guidelines for the execution of a will. It is better to spend an extra 10 minutes properly executing the will than to spend an extra 10 years litigating the issue as to whether it was properly signed. In most states, all adults are presumed to have testamentary capacity, and the burden of proving the contrary is on the person who contests the will.

What Law Governs Testamentary Capacity?

As to personal property, the laws of the state in which you reside govern. As to real property, the laws of the state in which the real estate is located govern. Generally, the disposition of property after death is controlled by the state laws and not the federal laws.

Prisoners

Ordinarily imprisonment does not destroy the right to make a will. In most of the states, it is provided by the constitution or by statute that conviction of a felony does not mean a forfeiture of an estate.

Illiterates

An illiterate person may execute a valid will if it is shown that he knows and understands the contents of his will, and if he meets the ordinary requirements of testamentary capacity.

Aged persons

Advanced age does not, in itself, prove the incapacity to make a will. Also physical and mental weaknesses, because of old age, do not prove incompetency. Where a contest occurs, however, these conditions will be considered along with other evidence, facts, and circumstances that surround the execution of the will.

Blind Persons

The fact that a person is blind does not affect his testamentary capacity. Particular care must be exercised in the execution of the will of a blind person to make certain that it accurately expresses his testamentary intention and that no imposition or deceit is practiced upon him.

Diseased Persons

Physical illness or infirmity does not render a person incapable of making a will. An invalid or a person physically weak or extremely nervous may designate who is to receive the property provided his mental capacity is not seriously impaired. Most ailments of the body to some extent affect the mind; but there is a vast difference between the mind distressed by physical pain and a mind which is devoid of reason. The mere lowering of mental vitality by physical suffering does not disqualify one from disposing of property.

Drug Addicts

Persons addicted to the use of drugs may dispose of their property by will. It must be shown, however, that this person had sufficient mind and memory to understand the nature of the property and the nature of the act at the time the will was executed.

Habitual Drunkards

Habitual or extreme intoxication does not in and of itself result in a person's incapacity. To invalidate a will there must be additional proof that at the time the will was executed the natural intelligence, memory, and judgment of the person writing the will were paralyzed or perverted because of the intoxication. Proof that the person was a habitual drunkard does not prove that person intoxicated at the time the will was written. It has been held that a person may be intoxicated and still possess sufficient capacity to execute a will; that is, if he is able to, and does comprehend the nature and effect of his act and recall the persons who are to receive the property.

Moral Depravity

Testamentary capacity is not dependent upon moral conduct. The fact that a person does not measure up to accepted moral standards does not invalidate a will so long as that person is sane and the will expresses a free intent and purpose.

Mental Capacity

Absolute soundness of mind is not essential for the valid execution of a will. Although it is not necessary that a person have an intellect measuring up to the ordinary standard of mankind, he must possess a certain amount of intelligence. The universal rule for the measurement of testamentary capacity is that the person must understand the nature of the instrument written, must be able to recollect who was designated to receive the property, must know the nature and extent of this property, and must be able to dispose of it according to a plan formed in his mind.

Insanity

Proof of insanity at the time a will is written nullifies the will. The degree of proof necessary to invalidate the will is difficult to determine in many cases. It is not medical soundness of mind that governs testamentary capacity but soundness of mind as defined by law. A court of law may declare a person insane and appoint a guardian for him. This alone is not conclusive proof of the incapacity to make a will. Neither is a person assumed to have testamentary capacity merely because the court decides that he or she no longer needs a guardian. A will, made by a person committed to an insane asylum, may be held valid if it can be shown that the will was written during an intelligible or lucid period.

Belief in spiritualism, mumbling incoherently, eccentricities and oddities are not automatic reasons for mental incapacity.

The neglect of personal hygiene and clothing, or offensive and disgusting habits are not necessarily considered evidence of insanity. A person who is vacillating, stubborn, stingy, easily angered, and indifferent to relatives does not necessarily demonstrate mental incapacity.

Unreasonable or unnatural provisions, unequal distribution among next of kin, and gifts to persons other than the natural recipients of a person's property do not constitute mental weakness unless they are so gross or ridiculous that they show obvious insanity. A person of sound mind may execute a will from any sort of motive that suits him or her, whether it be love, affection, gratitude, partiality, prejudice, hate, or capriciousness. Mental capacity is a question of fact to be decided by the court based upon all the evidence related to the issue. Many court battles have resulted from this issue.

Insane Delusions

An insane delusion, or false mental belief or conception that usually ignores reason, may or may not be of sufficient intensity to constitute mental incapacity. It must be established that the delusion directly affected the person's writing and that the belief expressed by that person was in fact false. An insane belief or a mere figment of the imagination (a belief in the existence of something which does not exist and which no rational person, in the absence of evidence, would believe to exist) are examples of delusions that can render wills invalid. To invalidate a will, the delusion must be a belief that is the spontaneous product of a diseased mind, that comes into existence without reason or evidence to support it, and that is adhered to against reason and against evidence.

A violent and unjust prejudice will not invalidate a will unless it is founded on an insane delusion. In one court case, a woman mistakenly believed that her relatives were unfriendly to her. The judge said that if all mistaken beliefs were to be cataloged as delusions, few indeed would escape the stigma of insanity. In another case, the judge said that if such belief is manifestly erroneous and entered into the will to the unjust detriment of the natural objects of the decedent's bounty, such belief amounts to a delusion such as renders the dece-

dent incapable of making a valid will. Mental incompetency
is not shown by the bequest of a person's estate to charity
simply because that person believed he could not otherwise
reach heaven. No creed or religious belief, in so far as it per-
tains to life after death, can be regarded as a delusion. This
is because there is no test by which this belief can be tried
or its truth or falsity demonstrated. Neither can a person's
erroneous views of the law be considered delusions that can
render a will void. If a belief is rational, though mistaken, it
is not an insane delusion.

Impaired Memory

A perfect memory is not a requisite to competency. A disposing memory has been defined as one in which a person can
recall the general nature, condition, and extent of his property and his relations to those to whom he gives and to those
from whom he withholds that property. Mere forgetfulness,
failure to recognize acquaintances, or failure to recollect the
names of friends has been held insufficient to establish mental incapacity. Failure of memory, unless complete or nearly
complete, does not invalidate a will.

Statutory Requirements

Generally, under modern statutes, a person of sound mind
and otherwise competent may dispose of his property according to his pleasure, unless in contravention of some statute
or common law rule. The general power of testamentary
disposition is founded on the assumption that a rational will
is a better disposition than any that can be made by the law
itself. Testamentary power involves a privilege under the law
to make a will while testamentary capacity concerns the ability
of the testator to make a will. By way of example, at common
law, convicts and married women had the capacity to make
a will, but were denied the power to make a will by the old
common law rules. Furthermore, statutes still require certain
age requirements before granting the power or right to make
a will. Each state has a statutory requirement as to the age

at which one is competent to make a will. The statutes vary from age fourteen to twenty-one. There is no rational explanation as to why a fourteen-year-old person in Georgia can legally make a will disposing of real estate while across the border in Alabama, one must be eighteen. It is, of course, obvious that many people under twenty-one years of age do not feel a strong need for a will; however, it is equally obvious that many people under the age of twenty-one may have an overriding need for executing a valid will. In all events, it is necessary to look to the specific statutes in each state to determine the legal age for making a will.

For 45 of the 50 states, the requirement is 18 years of age or older. Georgia is the only state that allows a person 14 years of age or older to legally execute a will. Alaska requires the age of 19 years or older. Three states define the age requirement with a term rather than a stated number of years: New Mexico (Majority), Vermont (Full Age) and Wyoming (Legal Age).

Who May Receive Property Under a Will?

The right to designate who receives property is a privilege granted to individuals by the various states. The states and the federal government have the power to tax the transfer of property. Taxes are levied on the transfer of assets and on those who receive the assets. Since a will is effective only upon death, the capacity of a legatee cannot be determined until that time. The capacity of a person receiving property at the time of death is ordinarily not destroyed by prior or subsequent incapacity. The law of the state in which real property is located governs the disposition of that real property by will. The law of the state in which the person who has been designated to receive that real property lives, governs the right to receive that property.

Husband and Wife

Most states have statutes that provide for dower, curtesy or statutory share (that portion of a person's property allowed to the spouse by statute). The rights of dower, curtesy or statutory share cannot be defeated by a will. A few states have recently abolished dower and curtesy but give a statutory share to the surviving spouse which is the same result. Most states also provide for a widow's allowance, homestead, and other rights which may not be defeated by a will. Subject to these statutory requirements, you may dispose of your property as you wish. If you become separated or divorced or your family situation changes in any way, it is very important that you review your will and change it accordingly. Most statutes provide that a divorce or marriage will change the effect of an existing will.

Adopted Children

If you have adopted someone, the adopted person may receive property through the will, and it makes no difference whether formal adoption has ever been established. It is only necessary that you clearly state your intention to devise or bequeath property to the adopted person. If the child, or adopted person, is specifically named to receive property, or when it appears by necessary implication that this person was meant to receive property, the instrument will be upheld. The recent trend in the laws is to treat the rights of adopted children the same as natural children.

Illegitimate Children

An illegitimate child may be given property by means of a will. If the child is not specifically named in the will, however, it must be clear that it is your intention to have the child included.

Murderer of the Testator

The right of a murderer to receive property by will from his victim has been denied by both civil law and common law. But few state courts in this country have made definite decisions on this issue, and the few decisions which have been made are unclear. To some extent, cases in this category are decided primarily on the specific facts and circumstances in each case. The statutory trend in most states is that a person who feloniously and intentionally kills another person may not inherit from that person. This is recommended by the Uniform Probate Code.

Attesting Witness or Spouse of Witness

Ordinarily, a person who witnesses and signs a will may not be a beneficiary of that will. This rule had its origin in the old common law of England and has been adopted in many of the states. Under the old English "Statute of Frauds," a person who witnessed a will was found to be incompetent, and the will was declared void because of incompetence. The injustice of this rule to the other beneficiaries of the will as well as to the person writing it soon became apparent, and the statutes were enacted restoring the competency of the witness but rendering this witness incapable of receiving property under the will. This removed the possibility of biased testimony as a witness could receive no financial gain. This rule is the reason for the suggested practice of not having any beneficiaries act as witnesses to your will.

In some states it has been held that only subscribing witnesses (those who sign as witnesses to the will) are barred from benefiting under the will, and not those who merely testify at probate as to the execution of the will or the capacity of the person who wrote it. Many statutes provide that if a will can be proved valid without the testimony of the witness who is to receive property, that witness may receive the property even though he testified at probate. In some states the right of a beneficiary, who is an essential witness to the will, is not destroyed but this beneficiary, or witness, may receive only that share of the estate he would be entitled to receive if there were no will. The amount, however, is not to exceed the amount to be given under the will.

By statutory provision in some states, property given to the wife or husband of a subscribing witness is void. The trend of the law is to permit the intent of the person writing the will whenever possible. In conclusion, it is best to choose as subscribing witnesses persons who are known to be trustworthy, but who have no financial stake in your will, either for themselves or their family.

Creditor of the Testator

A creditor of the person writing a will is not prohibited from accepting property by will from his debtor. However, when a creditor is a beneficiary under a will of his debtor, the question naturally arises as to whether the legacy was intended by the person writing the will in satisfaction of the debt and whether the creditor's acceptance of the legacy should bar his right to present the debt as a claim against the estate. This is a serious and complicated problem which is evidenced by the fact that the courts are in disagreement as to a general rule. In effect, it is your situation as expressed by the terms of your will or the circumstances surrounding its execution that governs. In the absence of unusual circumstances, a creditor may receive property under a will and also enforce a claim against the estate. A properly drafted will can avoid any dispute in these situations.

Debtor of the Testator

If you leave property to a person who owes you money, a similar question arises as to whether the property so willed cancels the debt. In the absence of an intention to the contrary, the property willed to a debtor will not, as a general rule, cancel the indebtedness. If you intend the willed property to cancel the indebtedness, this must be explicitly stated in the will, or it must be shown by competent evidence. In one case, where it was obvious by the terms of the will the testator intended the debtor to be the primary receiver of the property, the debt was not canceled because no specific direction was given in the will. The courts have held that the executor of a will may retain a sufficient amount of the estate property to satisfy any indebtedness of the estate. This rule is founded upon the principle that a debtor should not be allowed to receive his legacy while he retains possession of funds out of which his and other legacies are to be paid. A simple but specific direction in the will that a debt shall not be deducted from a legacy to the debtor is effective, and, conversely, a direction to deduct debts from the creditors' legacies is binding.

Corporations

A private corporation, being an artificial person, is generally qualified to receive property under a will. The right of a corporation to receive personal property by will is unquestioned and a bequest to a corporation for the future is valid. In most states, a corporation is permitted to take and hold real estate for the purposes for which it was incorporated.

Municipal Corporations

As a general rule a municipal corporation is capable of receiving a bequest either for its own use or in trust for a specific and proper purpose. A city, county, town, or school township have all been held proper beneficiaries under a will. Also, the United States is considered a corporation and may take property by will. Even a community in a foreign country may be a beneficiary under a will when permitted by the laws of that country to receive such property. The trend under most modern statutes is to permit almost any entity or person to receive property under a will.

Unincorporated Bodies

For the reason that property may be given only to persons capable in law of holding property, it is generally held that an unincorporated association may not take property by will; it is not a separate "entity" from its members. In some states an unincorporated association may be given either personal or real property. Sometimes a gift to an unincorporated body has been upheld as a gift to its incorporated parent body; this and other devices are used by the courts to comply with the intentions of the testator.

Disinheriting

Subject to your spouse's marital rights or to the terms of a valid contract you have with your spouse, you may, in most states, disinherit any or all of the persons who would have a claim to your estate in case there was no will. Although a parent ordinarily has the right to disinherit his children for any reason whatsoever, most of the states have provided by statute that the intention to disinherit a child must be clear.

By reason of the statutes, the omission of a child from a will is presumed to have been unintentional or due to mistake or forgetfulness. In some states extrinsic evidence to prove the intention to disinherit a child is admissible while in other states the intention must appear in the contents of the will. It is not essential that any specific provision be made in the will so long as the child is either named, or it can reasonably be implied that he was not forgotten.

Attorney Who Drafts Will

Most courts hold that a gift of property to the attorney who drafts your will presumes an improper or undue influence. This presumption is based upon the fact that people usually have a great deal of confidence, trust, and faith in their attorneys. The drafting of the will presents an opportunity and a temptation for the attorney, and this alone justifies the presumption. The presumption is one of fact and may be contested by competent evidence. Other courts simply hold that it violates professional ethics, or that it is otherwise wrong as against public policy.

Executor or Trustee

The executor of a will may receive property under the will; however, the bequest should be given to him clearly as an individual and not as executor, since it may otherwise be presumed that the gift is because of his capacity. Although it is generally stated that a bequest is given to a person as executor and not by name, or where the bequest is given on the condition that the person enters upon and fulfills the duties of executor, the courts will presume that the legacy was given in a representative capacity and not the individual, and therefore was intended to be in place of compensation. Bequests to a trustee of a living trust have been generally upheld as valid, and are authorized and are approved by most modern state statutes.

The Uniform Probate Code

The National Conference of Commissioners on Uniform State Laws adopted a Uniform Probate Code and has recommended it to the various states to help make the laws more uniform. This modern code was approved by the American Bar Association and has been adopted, in whole or in part, by several states. It is anticipated that the Code will be adopted by most of the states in the future. The Code is based on the proposition that laws relating to probate and trust proceedings, minors, and certain oher persons whose circumstances make protection of their persons or property desirable should be modernized and made uniform throughout the country. The Code consists of eight Articles, the second of which includes the descent and distribution of property and the writing of wills.

The purposes and policies of the Code are:

- To simplify and clarify the laws concerning the affairs of decedents, missing persons, protected persons, minors, and incapacitated persons.
- To discover and make effective the intent of a decedent in the distribution of his property.
- To promote a speedy and efficient system for liquidating the estate of the decedent and making distribution to the persons entitled to the property.
- To facilitate the use and enforcement of certain trusts.
- To make uniform the laws among the various states.

The Code simplifies the use of certified and authenticated copies of death certificates and other official documents. It also provides that a person who is absent for a continuous period of 5 years, during which he has not been heard from and whose absence is not satisfactorily explained after diligent search or inquiry, is presumed to be dead. His death is presumed to have occurred at the end of that period unless there is sufficient evidence to determine that death occurred earlier. This is a change from the old common law rule of seven years.

The purposes of Article II of the Code are:

- To provide an acceptable estate plan for persons who fail to plan for themselves.
- To provide a procedure by which an individual can more easily control the distribution of his assets or estates.
- To provide clear statutory rules that govern areas where oversights by testators may be anticipated.

These changes in the statutes will make it much easier for you to draft a will. The Code abolishes the distinction between real and personal property, and provides that all property not disposed of by the will passes to the heirs in the same manner. The Code attempts to reflect the normal desire of the owner of property as to the disposition of his property at death. These provisions are based upon conclusions reached after extensive studies and analyses of many wills that have been filed for probate.

The principle features of the Code, which attempt to provide for the disposition of property as the owner would have wanted, are the following:

- A large share is given to the surviving spouse, if there are children, and the whole estate if there are no children or parent(s).
- Inheritance by collateral relatives is limited to grandparents and those descended from grandparents. This simplifies proof of heirship and eliminates will contests by remote relatives.
- An heir must survive the decedent for five days in order to qualify under the statute. This is an extension of the reasoning behind the Uniform Simultaneous Death Act and is similar to provisions found in many wills.
- Adopted children are treated as children of the adopting parents for all inheritance purposes and cease to be children of natural parents. This reflects modern policy of recent statutes and court decisions.
- In an era when *inter vivos* gifts (gifts during one's lifetime) are frequently made within the family, it is unrealistic

to preserve the *concepts of advancement* clause which was written when such gifts were rare. The statute provides that gifts during a lifetime are not advancements unless declared or acknowledged in writing.

The *intestate estate* is defined in the Code as any part of the estate of a decedent not effectively disposed of by decedent's will. This estate passes to the heirs as prescribed in the Code.

It is provided in the Code that any person who fails to survive the decedent by 120 hours (5 days) is deemed to have predeceased the decedent for purposes of homestead allowance, exempt property, and intestate succession. The decedent's heirs are determined on that basis. If the time of death of the decedent or of the person who would otherwise be an heir, or the times of death of both, cannot be determined, and it cannot be established that the person who would otherwise be an heir has survived the decedent by 120 hours, it is deemed that the person failed to survive for the required period. This provision, however, is not to be applied where its application would result in the taking of intestate estate by the state under the *escheat laws* (reverting to the state).

The Code contains an optional provision preventing a felonious and intentional killer from inheriting from his victim, and providing that the estate of the decedent passes as if the killer had predeceased him. Other parts of the Code disqualify the killer from taking, by right of survivorship, property owned in joint tenancy, or as beneficiary of a life insurance policy, bond, or other contractual arrangement, or any other property. A final judgment of conviction of felonious and intentional killing is conclusive for purposes hereof, but in the absence of such a conviction the court may determine by a preponderance of evidence whether the killing was felonious and intentional.

The Code abolishes the common law estates of dower and curtesy. This reflects modern thinking in the share of the intestate estate to be given to a surviving spouse. It also provides sufficient protection against disinheritance of the surviving spouse. Under the Code, the estate share to be given to the surviving spouse is:

- The entire intestate estate if there is no surviving child or parent of the decedent.
- The first $50,000 plus one-half of the balance of the estate if there is no surviving child but the decedent is survived by a parent or parents.
- The first $50,000 plus one-half of the balance of the estate if there are surviving children all of whom are children of the surviving spouse.
- One-half of the intestate estate if there are surviving children, one or more of whom are not children of the surviving spouse.

This section of the Code gives the surviving spouse a larger share than most existing statutes. In doing so, it reflects the desires of most married persons, who almost always leave all of a moderate estate or at least one-half of a larger estate to the surviving spouse. A husband or wife who desires to leave the surviving spouse less than the share provided by this section may do so in the will, except that the surviving spouse may, under the Code, elect to take a one-third share.

A spouse who fails to survive the decedent by 120 hours will be considered, under the Code, to have predeceased the decedent and will not be entitled to the intestate share of a surviving spouse.

Under the Code, the intestate estate which does not pass to a surviving spouse passes to the *lineal descendants* (child, grandchild, great-grandchild, and so on) of the decedent, parents of the decedent and their descendants, or grandparents of the decedent and distant relatives descended from grandparents. Persons in the ascending line more remote than grandparents and distant relatives descending from a common ancestor more remote than grandparents, are eliminated from the group of heirs who can take from an intestate. The elimination of these remotely related persons is in line with modern policy as evidenced by the most recent drafts of probate codes in various states.

For purposes of intestate succession under the Code, an adopted child is the child of the adopting parent and is not treated as a child of the natural parent. Relatives of the decedent, conceived before death but born thereafter, inherit under the Code as if they had been born in the lifetime of the decedent. No person is disqualified as an heir because he is or has been an alien. This provision is compatible with a recent United States Supreme Court decision based on constitutional grounds. If there are no takers under the provisions of the Code, the intestate estate passes to the state.

The Code assures the surviving spouse of a share in both the probate estate and certain assets transferred outside of the probate process. The decedent cannot defeat this provision. This elective share takes the place of common law dower and curtesy, which are abolished by the Code. It provides the surviving spouse with a right to take an elective share of one-third of the *augmented estate*. The right of a surviving spouse to take an elective share under the Code is a personal right and may be exercised by the spouse only during his lifetime.

The *Uniform Simultaneous Death Act*, enacted in all states, provides that where the title to, or passage of, property depends on priority of death and evidence that the persons involved died other than simultaneously is insufficient, the property of each person should, with certain exceptions, be disposed of as if each had survived. An appropriate provision in your will eliminates these problems. Even though the Uniform Probate Code requires that one must survive the decedent by 5 days to take property under the Code, it is recommended that you consider increasing this period to 30 days, 60 days, or even 6 months. This avoids the possibility of the probate of your estate (including tax liabilities) and another probate of the same assets (including tax liabilities) through the estate of any of your survivors who may survive you for only a short period of time.

Federal Estate
and Gift Taxes

Before the enactment of the Economic Tax Recovery Act of 1981 many estate planning and will writing efforts were directed toward the avoidance of federal estate and gift taxes. The new Tax Code provided much more liberal exemptions. After 1986 each individual exemption will be $600,000. Moreover, there is an unlimited marital deduction. Therefore, over 99% of the estates will be exempt from such taxes. In view of these significant changes in the tax laws many people can write their own wills without having to worry about these tax problems.

The federal estate tax is imposed on the transfer of an individual's property at his death and on certain other transfers deemed to be the equivalent of transfers at death. The tax is imposed on the *taxable estate*. This is the value of the total property transferred or considered transferred at death. It is the gross estate reduced by various deductions, such as expenses, debts, claims, taxes and losses, marital deductions, charitable deductions, etc.

The tax is computed under the unified rate schedule applicable to both gift and estate taxes. Under the unified rate structure, lifetime gifts and transfers at death are taxed on a cumulative basis. Under the new tax code, estate taxes generally do not become a factor until the taxable estate exceeds the new exemption amounts. These amounts and the years in which they were phased in appear in the preface. Remember that an unlimited amount can be transferred to a spouse, before or after death, without estate or gift taxes. This means that very few estates will have any estate and gift tax problems.

There is now a $10,000 annual exclusion for gifts which means that any taxpayer may make gifts to any number of donees per year up to $10,000 each with no gift or estate tax liability.

The main category of property included in a decedent's gross estate is that in which the decedent had full or partial ownership when he died. Certain transfers made during the donor's lifetime, without adequate and full compensation, are taxed as part of the donor's gross estate for tax purposes because they are considered to be testamentary in nature. Gifts made within three years of the donor's death, gifts not taking full effect before the donor's death, and gifts which the donor may modify may be drawn into the donor's estate except to the extent that such transfers were made for adequate and full compensation.

Writing Your Own Will

To review, the essential elements of a will are: a written instrument, a competent testator, an intent to dispose of property after death, and a will that is executed in accordance with statutory requirements. Obviously, a will contains much more than these elements and is limited only by the specific needs and desires of the person who writes it.

Although it is not absolutely essential to make a current inventory of your assets before writing your will, it is advisable to do so. The usual inventory includes such items as real estate, cash, automobiles, tangible personal property, stocks, bonds, insurance, profit sharing and pension funds, mutual funds, loans owed to you, business interests, and miscellaneous items. An essential part of estate planning consists of knowing the nature and extent of your current assets. After preparing your inventory of assets, you will find it much easier to make a decision as to what dispositions you wish to make in your will.

Do You Need a Lawyer to Write Your Will?

You do not need a lawyer to write a will unless you have significant tax problems or other legal entanglements. However, if you have any feelings of trepidation or uncertainty about your being able to write your own will, it is recommended that you consult with your attorney. Even if you decide to retain a lawyer for writing your own will, you can save money by completing your own inventory of assets and drafting your own version of your will to be reviewed by your attorney.

When Should You Retain a Lawyer?

Any time you are unsure about your own ability to properly write your own will, or having any legal problems, you should consult with your lawyer. It is much better to go to the trouble and expense of consulting a lawyer before you have a legal emergency than after it is too late. There are instances where it is advisable to consult a competent attorney in a timely fashion, to save money, time, embarassment and frustration.

The Main Parts of a Will

The following discussion will provide a checklist of the specific subjects usually found in a will and cover each of these subjects to the extent necessary to prepare a will. It will also provide examples of specific language to accomplish your objectives. It will present examples of typical wills that should cover all your needs. In drafting a will, you should use straightforward, commonly understood words and phrases. Avoid any terms that are ambiguous or subject to misunderstandings. If a phrase, sentence, or paragraph is not clear in its meaning, when it is written, it surely may be misinterpreted later. You should write simply but precisely in stating your intentions. You should describe the specific results you want to accomplish. The more you know about wills and how the courts interpret them, the better prepared you will be to draft one of your own. The typical will usually contains the following parts:

- Introductory or Publication Clause
- Special Instructions
- Appointment of Executor, Executrix, Trustee or Guardian
- General Gifts
- Specific Gifts
- Residuary Clause
- Execution of Will (Testimonium Clause)
- Attestation Clause
- Signatures and Addresses of Witnesses
- Self Proof of Will

It is not mandatory that the contents be in any particular order, except that your signature and the signatures of the witnesses should be located at the end of the instrument. It is more convenient to have appointment of the executor or executrix on the first page, especially if you have a long will. If you will is longer than one page, it is good practice to sign in the margin on each page as well as on the last page. The signature at the end of the will is the only one that must be witnessed. The pages should be fastened together securely. It is recommended that the material be spaced so that the closing parts of the will—the testimonium clause, signature, attestation clause, and the witnesses' signatures—appear on the same page. Careful study of this book will better enable you to select, from the forms, the language necessary for a draft of your own will.

These basic will forms are used by most of the people who write wills. In fact, unless your estate exceeds the exemption amounts or you have some special estate problem, one of these basic wills is preferred. With the use of these forms and the additional provisions contained in the appendix, you should have no difficulty in drafting your will. If you are one of the few who has estate tax implications or other special situations, it is appropriate and proper to obtain professional assistance. If you decide to consult a professional, the knowledge gained from reading this book will save you and your professional consultant a lot of time, a factor that should lower fees.

Introductory or Publication Clause

This is the part that identifies the testator. It states that this is your last will and testament and that you are of sound mind and memory. It may be used to revoke all prior wills, if any. Here are the usual phrases used:

Example 1: I, John Doe, of the City of _____, State of _____, being of sound and disposing mind and memory, do make, publish and declare this to be my Last Will and Testament, and hereby revoke all former wills and codicils by me made.

Example 2: I, John Doe, being of sound and disposing mind and memory and hereby intending to dispose of all property belonging to me at my death, of whatever kind and wherever situated, do make, publish and declare this to be my Last Will and Testament...

Example 3: I, John Doe, of _____ (Address) _____, City of _____, State of _____, make this my Last Will and revoke all prior wills and codicils.

Special Instructions

The law imposes a legal obligation to pay debts, and although it is not necessary to include a statement on the debts, such a statement is usually found in most wills. When a surviving spouse is obligated to pay the burial expenses of a deceased spouse, it can make a difference in the administration of the estate. This is a question you should discuss fully with your family when preparing your will. It is unnecessary to give specific directions about burial instructions, but this is another question you may wish to discuss with your family. Actually this should be done by separate written instructions and not as a part of your will. Because of the high costs associated with a typical funeral, many people now give specific directions to avoid excessive expenses. Instructions for cremation and donation to research foundations seem to be the current trend among people in this country. The typical provisions are:

Example 1: My executor, hereinafter named, shall give my body a burial suitable to the wishes of my relatives and friends, and pay all of my funeral expenses, together with all my just debts, out of the first moneys coming into my estate.

Example 2: I direct that I be interred in a plot owned by me in_____cemetery in the City of _____, State of _____, more particularly known as _____ (legal description) _____, and that a suitable headstone be erected and inscribed upon said lot. The total cost of my funeral including the headstone shall be upwards of _____ Dollars, and for the purpose of providing for the perpetual care of said plot in said cemetery I hereby give, devise and bequeath to said cemetery, its successors and assigns the sum of _____ Dollars.

Example 3: It is my wish and I direct that my body shall be cremated after my death.

Appointment of Executor, Executrix, Trustee, or Guardian

Who should you appoint as executor or executrix of your will? Who should be appointed guardian of minor children or trustee of any trust you may establish? These are important questions and should receive careful consideration. The answers to these questions will depend entirely upon your own particular situation. The following general rules and suggestions will be helpful.

If you have a relatively small estate, you may wish to designate your spouse, a close relative, or a good friend to be the executor or executrix, the guardian of your children, or the trustee of your trusts. If there are no extensive business activities involved, no complicated real estate transactions, and no other major complications, these appointments are generally satisfactory and usually result in no difficulties and may reduce the amounts incurred for administration expenses. If a relatively large estate consists primarily of liquid assets or assets which can easily be converted to liquid assets, such appointments are also satisfactory. Moreover, the more family members do in the probate of an estate, the more the savings of probate expenses and attorney's fees.

Where an estate has a substantial interest in an active business necessitating active participation, complex partnership interests, extensive real estate holdings, or other assets which require active management and participation, it may be advisable to appoint someone with business experience.

If you have minor children, or close relatives who are minors or otherwise unable to handle their own business affairs, you may set up a trust and designate a trustee to administer the trust until the beneficiaries become adults. The same general principles apply to the appointment of a guardian with the exception that when possible and appropriate, it is usually preferable to have an adult relative appointed guardian of very young children. You cannot always assume that the guardian of your minor children will be your surviving spouse. Simultaneous deaths are not uncommon. These questions should be carefully considered, and you will want to discuss them with your family. Your personal choice will usually be better than an appointment made by some judge who may not know you or your relatives.

After making these appointments you should select alternates as successors to these appointments. There is no assurance that the person you designate at first will be able to act, or that the designated person will survive you. You should also carefully consider whether to waive bonds. This is generally recommended to save costs and expenses assuming, of course, that you have confidence in your appointees. Some suggested forms follow.

Example 1: I hereby appoint Tom Doe of the City of _____, State of _____, and The First National Bank of ___(city, state)___, executors of this my Last Will and Testament.

Example 2: I hereby appoint Tom Doe of the City of __, State of _____, executor of this my Last Will and Testament, and direct that no bond or other undertaking be required of him for the faithful performance of the duties of his office.

Example 3: I appoint Tom Doe Executor hereunder and if he shall fail to qualify, or having qualified shall die, resign, or cease to act as Executor, then I appoint John Jones to act hereunder. No Executor named herein shall be required to give bond.

Example 4: (Guardian) If it shall be necessary to appoint a guardian for any minor child of mine, I appoint Tom Doe as such guardian. If he shall fail to qualify, or having qualified, shall die, resign, or cease to act as such guardian, then I appoint John Jones to serve as such guardian.

General Gifts

General legacies are usually in money, but may be in other forms of personal property.

Example 1: I give and bequeath to Mark Doe the sum of Fifty Thousand Dollars ($50,000.00).

Example 2: I give and bequeath to Mark Doe fifty (50) shares of common stock of A.T. & T.

Specific Gifts

Specific gifts are of particular personal property which is specifically designated; for example, items as jewelry, antiques, art objects, and other tangible objects.

Example 1: I give and bequeath my white pearl pin to my son, Tom Doe.

Example 2: I give and bequeath any automobile I may own at the time of my death to my son, Tom Doe.

Residuary Clauses

The residuary clause can be a very important part of a will — or it can be of no significance. That is, if there is nothing left in the estate it is of no significance. On the other hand, if a person has a large estate, the residuary clause would cover the diposition of all of the estate not specifically treated in the other provisions of the will. In the event a beneficiary of a general or specific bequest predeceases you that property would generally become a part of the residuary estate.

Example 1: All the rest, residue, and remainder of my property, real, personal, and mixed, at whatever time acquired by me and wherever situated, I give, devise, and bequeath to _____ .
(name)

Example 2: I give the residue of my estate to my wife Jane.

Execution of Will

The courts do not have the power to add to, or subtract from, the statutory requirements that govern the signing of a will. As the testator, your intention in this regard is also of no importance. You must comply with the requirements of your state statute.

The written will must be signed in some way by you and, to be valid, must be witnessed by competent persons. The only allowable exceptions are the rather unusual procedures previously mentioned (holographic wills and nuncupative wills).

You may personally subscribe your name, make your mark, have another person write your name for you, or have another person guide your hand or affix your fingerprint. Practically any court will hold that the will is valid if you affix your mark instead of write your name. The signature by a third party is sufficient if made in your presence, at your direction, and you assent to and adopt such signature as your own. If you are physically unable to sign your name, you may seek assistance from another person to help you write your name. As long as you participate in the act of signing your name and adopt it as your signature, the will is valid.

Frequent reference has been made to the signing of a will in accordance with statutory requirements. It is essential that you strictly comply with the requirements of any statute which may govern the disposition of property. You should take precautions when signing your will to avoid the mistakes that have generated will contests in the past.

Here is a recommended procedure to follow in the execution and attestation of a will.

Prepare the final draft of the will, preferably on a typewriter or other printing facility, with an original and one or more copies. Type the attestation clause in the proper place. Allow ample space for your signature and the signatures of the witnesses. Number the pages and bind them together firmly. Make certain that you thoroughly understand the meaning of every part of the will.

Bring the witnesses together. Three witnesses will satisfy the requirements in all states except Louisiana. The witnesses should not be beneficiaries under the will or spouses of a beneficiary.

Inform the witnesses that the document before them is your last will. It is not necessary or even desirable that they be allowed to read it. Then you should state that you are about to sign the will and request the witnesses to witness your signature.

Then, with all the witnesses observing your action, sign the will. You should sign only the original; the carbon copies, as a matter of good practice, remain unsigned but conformed. After you sign the will say to the witnesses, "This is my signature and this is my will. Will you please sign as attesting witnesses?"

Next, have the witnesses read the attestation clause. Then, have each witness sign immediately below the attestation clause and write his address. Neither you nor any of the witnesses should leave the room until all have signed the document. Each signature must be observed by you and all the other witnesses.

Now the document is a will. The signed original should be placed in a safe place where it is available to you and to the executor. Do not place it in a safety deposit vault because a court order may be required to get it out. The unsigned copies should be conformed by typing or writing in the information from the original and placed in a different safe place.

Three witnesses are required by the statutory requirements of New Hampshire, South Carolina, and Vermont. All other states except Louisiana require only two witnesses. The holographic will, legal in 23 states, needs no witnesses.

It is ordinarily required by most of the statutes that the witnesses be competent or credible. A competent witness has been defined as a person who could, at the time of attesting to the will, legally testify in court to the facts to which he attests by subscribing his name to the will. Credible is ordinarily used in the same sense as competent.

Attestation Clause

While most states require only two witnesses to a will, it is desirable to have at least three. Witnesses who are permanent residents of your city are preferable and their addresses should always appear on the will.

The attestation clause is not, by legal definition, a part of the will. It follows the will and is the written and signed statement of the witnesses. Its use is strongly recommended because it is strong evidence that the will has been properly prepared. It serves as an authoritative memorandum to refresh the memories of the witnesses. It is a good practice to include a statement that all the statutory requirements have been complied with. It is also recommended practice to state the number of pages in the will. If there have been any erasures or corrections in the will (and there should not be), they should be referred to in the attestation clause making it clear that the erasures or corrections were made by you before you signed the will. Typical attestation clauses follow.

Example 1: The foregoing instrument, consisting of three (3) typewritten pages, including this page, was signed, sealed, published, and declared by the said John Doe as his Last Will and Testament, in the presence of each of us, who at his request and in his presence and in the presence of one another, subscribe our names hereto as witnesses on the day of the date hereof; and we declare that at the time of the execution of this instrument the said John Doe, according to our best knowledge and belief, was of sound and disposing mind and memory and under no constraint.

Example 2: Signed, sealed, published, and declared by John Doe, the above named testator, who appears to us to be of sound and disposing mind and memory, as and for his Last Will and Testament in our presence, and we, at his request, in his presence and in the presence of each other, have hereunto subscribed our names as witnesses this_____day of_____, 19_____.

Self Proof of Will

A procedural device for the easy proof of wills has been adopted in most states. This procedure is recommended by the Uniform Probate Code and will probably be adopted by all states in the future. It is a further modernization and simplification of the probate procedures. It can be used as proof of a will without having to call in witnesses to do so after death, except in cases of contested wills. The self proof of a will may be made when the will is being written or subsequent to that time. As the testator, your acknowledgment of the will and the affidavits of the witnesses are made before an officer who is authorized to administer oaths. That person's authority is evidenced by the certificate attached to or following the will. This procedure is not required or necessary, but it is recommended that you use it if a notary public or other authorized official is available at the execution of the will. It may save a great deal of time, expenses, and effort, and it adds to the formality of the will.

A suggested form of the Self Proof of Will acknowledgment is as follows:

Self Proof of Will

STATE OF _____

                                                                            ss

COUNTY OF _____

We, _____(name)_____, _____(name)_____, _____(name)_____, and _____(name)_____, the testator and the witnesses respectively, whose names are signed to the attached or foregoing instrument, were sworn and declared to the under-signed officer that the testator signed the instrument as his last will, that he signed, and that each of the witnesses, in the presence of the testator and in the presence of each other, signed the will as a witness.

(Signature)	*(Signature)*
Testator	Witness
	(Signature)
	Witness
	(Signature)
	Witness

Subscribed and sworn to before me by ____*(name)*____, *the testator, and by* ____*(name)*____, ____*(name)*____ *and* *(name)*, *the witnesses on the* _____ *day of* _____, 19 ____.

My Commission Expires:

_____*(date)*_____	*(Signature)*_____
	Notary Public

An *acknowledgment* is a public declaration or formal statement of the person executing an instrument made to the official authorized to make the acknowledgment, that the execution of the instrument was his free act and deed. It is written evidence of an acknowledgment which generally states and declares that the person named in the document was known to the official and appeared before him and acknowledged the instrument to be his act and deed. An *affidavit* is a written statement made voluntarily and sworn to or affirmed before a person legally authorized to administer an oath or affirmation. As a general rule, any person who has knowledge of the facts sworn to in the writing may make an affidavit.

As a general rule, officers authorized to take acknowledgments include judges, clerks of court, notaries public, commissioners, and justices of the peace. Each state has a statute that makes these designations. In foreign countries the authorized officials usually include judges of a court of record, diplomatic counselors or commercial agents of the United States, and notaries public. Certain designated military personnel have authority to administer oaths for purpose of military administration, including military justice, and to act as notary and United States Consul in the performance of all notarial acts to be executed by members of the armed forces.

Miscellaneous Clauses

There are a number of other items that may be appropriate for certain wills. Each is examined in detail in the following sections.

Forgiveness of Debts

If you wish to forgive a specific debt owed to you by a person whom you designate as a beneficiary under your will, make a specific statement in the will of this intention. If you intend for the debt to be deducted from the legacy, state such an intent in the will.

Example: I give and bequeath to Mark Manning the sum of Five Thousand ($5,000.00) Dollars. I release and discharge said Mark Manning of any and all outstanding debts and interest thereon due me from him at the time of my death, and direct that the said Five Thousand ($5,000.00) Dollars be paid to the said Mark Manning in full, without any deduction on account of such indebtedness.

Common Disaster Clause

It is depressing enough to contemplate your own death, but the remote possibility of common disasters should be considered in the preparation of your will. Common disasters or simultaneous deaths are unfortunate, but it is equally unfortunate to see an estate shrink in size by being probated two or three times within a few years. It is one of the primary objectives of a good will to avoid unnecessary taxes and administration expenses. A common disaster clause or simultaneous death clause, as in the following examples, can help achieve this objective.

Example 1: If any beneficiary and I should die in a common accident or disaster, or if any beneficiary dies within 30 (60, 90) days of my death, then all the provisions of this will shall take effect as if such beneficiary had in fact predeceased me.

Example 2: In the event that any beneficiary under this my will and I shall die under such circumstances that there is no sufficient evidence that we died otherwise than simultaneously, such beneficiary shall be deemed to have predeceased me.

Codicils

A codicil is an instrument that either adds to, or changes, an existing will. A codicil, to be valid, must meet all the statutory requirements of a will. In most instances, a codicil is merely a temporary change of a will until the testator has time to rewrite the entire will. Significant or extensive changes usually should not be made by codicil. It is recommended that you prepare a new will instead of relying upon codicils unless there is some compelling reason not to rewrite the will. For example, if a person is nearing senility or incapacity it is not recommended to write a new will, but to make a codicil for any changes. In most other instances, it will be as easy to write a new will as to write a codicil.

Revocation of Wills

To revoke a will means to annul it in whole or in part. A revocation may be expressed by virtue of a revocation clause contained in a later will or implied by reason of an inconsistent disposition of property in a later will. Under some statutes, a change in the circumstances of the testator subsequent to the execution of the will may constitute a revocation by operation of law. This emphasizes the importance of reviewing your will periodically, or after any significant change in your circumstances, to assure yourself that your will meets with your desires and intention. Upon being revoked, a testamentary provision ceases to exist, and is inoperative as if it had never been written.

A will may be revoked by tearing it up, cutting, burning, cancellation, erasure, obliteration, and any other physical act which essentially destroys the will so long as the acts are intended by you, the testator, as a revocation. A will may be revoked by operation of law, or as it is sometimes called *revocation implied by law*. Such a revocation may result from certain circumstances not specifically mentioned in the statutes which prescribe the proper methods of revocation. The doctrine is that the revocation of a will can be implied by certain changes in your family, domestic relations, your property, or one of the beneficiaries of your will. By these actions the law infers or presumes that you intended to make the change. The intended change may be either total or partial. The rule is based on the theory that by reason of such changes subsequent to the date of the will, you have acquired new moral duties and obligations. Subsequent marriage or divorce may have a significant change in the will. The death of the sole beneficiary in effect abrogates the will. Changes in the character of the estate will change the effect of a will. The birth of additional children could have an effect on an existing will.

Although most people rarely revoke a will without immediately preparing another, it is important for you to be familiar with the changes imposed by law so you will be in a position to prepare your own will and change it from time to time to meet your special needs.

Checklist

The final step in being able to draft a will is to assemble all of the facts and information about your estate, family, and personal situation. This is very important because it clearly defines your personal situation and enables you to answer questions. The following checklist is designed to assist you in collecting facts you need. As you compile the information and identify each item that should be covered in the will, you can turn to the forms and draft an appropriate provision to resolve the question.

Name of Testator (your name)
- Are you known by any other name?
- Have you used other names in the past?
- If a name change has occurred, are the legal papers in order?

Domicile
- Do you own or maintain a residence outside the state in which the will is to be executed?
- Should a definitive statement be made in the will as to your intent regarding domicile or residence?

Age
- Do the dates on birth certificates and insurance policies coincide?
- Is evidence of your birthdate sufficient for social security purposes?

Family
- Are you married, single, a widow, widower, or adopted?
- Any previous marriages?
- What are the names, addresses, ages, and marital status of your children?
- Are there any adopted children?
- Are there any deceased children?
- Do you intend to disinherit any of your children?
- Are any provisions to be made for children born after your death?
- Are any provisions to be made for individuals who claim to be your children?
- Have advancements been made to any of the children?
- If so, are they to be deducted from the gifts to the children?

- Are your parents living?
- Do you want to provide for them?
- Do you want to provide for any grandchildren?
- Do you want to provide for any other relatives?

Guardian

- Do you want a guardian to be appointed for your minor children?
- If so, who shall be appointed?
- Is the guardian to be required to give bond?
- What provision should be made for the support of your children?

Funeral Instructions

- Do you have a preference as to how your body should be disposed of?
- Are any provisions regarding cemetery lot, tombstone, and upkeep of the cemetery lot to be provided for in the will?

Prior Wills and Codicils

- Do you have copies of prior wills and codicils?
- Are all prior wills and codicils to be revoked?
- Have you made provisions to destroy any prior wills?

Debts

- Do you have any existing debts?
- Do you have any liability, such as surety on a bond, pledge to any charity or the like, etc.?
- Are debts to be paid from any specific property?
- What property is mortgaged or has other liens?
- Is mortgage or lien to be paid by the person or persons who receive your property, from the general estate or from a particular fund?
- What property is to be sold first to pay any debts of the estate?
- If a gift is made to a creditor, is it to be in payment of your indebtedness or an addition thereto?

Debts Owed to You

- Are any debts to be cancelled?
- Are special provisions to be made for their payment?
- If a legacy is given to one who is indebted to you, is the debt to be deducted from that legacy?

Husband and Wife

- Was an antenuptial agreement made?
- Are gifts to be in lieu of dower or curtesy?
- Are gifts to stop if the surviving spouse remarries?
- Are family living expenses to be provided during the period of time when the estate is being settled?

Property Owned by You

- Is there any property in your name that belongs to someone else?
- What is to be done with your property which is held as an agent or trustee for another?
- What property is to be specifically bequeathed or devised and to whom?
- What is to be done with your business, if any?
- What property is held jointly?
- Have you created any living trust?
- Have you any future or contingent interest? If so, how is it to be disposed of?
- Real Property

    What real property do you own?

    Is the property owned in fee simple?

    Has any real property been bought or sold on contract for deed?

    Is any of this property mortgaged?

    If mortgaged, is the devise to be subject to the mortgage?

    Is there any real property located outside the state where you live?

    What real property is to be specifically devised and to whom?

    In whose name is the title to your family home?

- Personal Property
  What specific items are to be bequeathed and to whom?
  What money legacies, if any, are to be made and to whom?
  How are personal effects to be disposed of?
  Are any particular stocks, bonds, or mortgages to be specifically bequeathed? To whom?

- Partnership Property
  Are you a member of any partnership?
  Are there articles of partnership?
  What provision is to be made as to the disposition of the interest in the partner and partnership?

Residuary Clause
- What shall be done with the balance of estate after all bequests have been paid or devised of real estate made or trusts set up and all debts paid?

Trusts
- Is any of your property to be left in trust?
- Who is to be the appointed trustee?
- What is to be done if the trustee dies, resigns, or is unable to act?
- To whom is the income to be paid and how is the principal to be distributed?

Conditional Gifts
- Are any gifts to be conditional?
- Are any provisions to be made for disinheriting persons who may contest the will?

Charities
- What gifts, if any, are to be given to charities?
- What gifts, if any, are to be given to servants, employees or other persons?

Executor
- Who is to be the executor?
- Are provisions made if the executor decides or refuses to act as such?
- Will the executor be required to give bond?

Will Forms and Alternative Will Provisions

You can write your own will in the privacy of your own home without a lawyer and have the satisfaction of knowing your estate won't be distributed pursuant to a state statute, maybe even to strangers, but will go to those you designate. In this way, there will be no lawyers or others meddling in your private affairs. As previously mentioned, making your own will can also save money, time, frustration and a lot of the unnecessary aggravation of the probate system.

Before writing your will, you should read this entire book and then review the sections that pertain to your individual situation.

In preparing to write your own will you should make an inventory of your family assets, study the checklist, and discuss will writing with other members of your family. If the forms that follow do not contain exactly what you need, you should have no difficulty in selecting the form that most closely fits your situation and then take items from the other will forms, or from the list of alternative provisions, and be able to cover all your needs.

Two important considerations in writing your will are to spell everything out clearly, leaving nothing to chance, and periodically reviewing your will and other estate plans.

WILL FORM 1: Husband: Entire Estate to Wife If She Survives; Otherwise to Others

LAST WILL AND TESTAMENT
OF
(name)

I *(name)*, a resident of *(city)*, *(state)*, hereby publish this my Last Will and Testament and revoke all prior wills and codicils.

1. Special Instructions: I direct that all my legal debts and funeral expenses be paid as soon as practicable after my death.

2. Disposition: I give my entire estate to my wife *(name)* if she survives me. If she does not survive me, I give my entire estate (in equal shares) to the following beneficiary or beneficiaries who survive me: _____
_____ .

3. Trust for Minors, If Any: The share of any beneficiary who shall be under the age of 18 (21, 25) years shall not be paid to such beneficiary but shall instead be held in trust to apply to his/her use all the income thereof, and also such amounts of the principal, even to the extent of all, as my Trustee deems necessary or suitable for the support, welfare and education of such beneficiary; and, when he/she attains the age of 18 (21, 25) years, to pay him/her the remaining principal, if any. If any beneficiary for whom a share is held in trust should die before having received all the principal thereof, then upon his/her death the remaining principal shall be paid to his/her then living child or children, equally if more than one, and in default thereof, to my then living descendants, per stirpes.

4. Executor: I appoint my wife, _____ *(name)* _____, executrix hereunder and if she shall fail to qualify, or having qualified shall die, resign, or cease to act as Executrix, then I appoint _____ *(name)* _____ to act hereunder. No Executrix or Executor named herein shall be required to give bond.

5. Guardian: If it shall be necessary to appoint a guardian for any minor child of mine, I appoint _____ *(name)* _____ as such guardian. If he shall fail to qualify, or having qualified, shall

die, resign, or cease to act as such guardian, then I appoint
___*(name)*___ to serve as such guardian.

6. Trustee: In the event any trust shall come into existence
under this will, I appoint ___*(name)*___ as Trustee hereunder.
If he shall fail to qualify, or having qualified, shall die, resign
or cease to act for any reason, I appoint ___*(name)*___ to act as
such Trustee. No Trustee named herein shall be required to
give bond.

7. Simultaneous Death Clause: If any beneficiary and I
should die in a common accident or disaster, or if any
beneficiary dies within 30 (60, 90) days of my death, then all
the provisions of this will shall take effect as if such beneficiary
had in fact predeceased me.

IN WITNESS WHEREOF, I have hereunto set my hand this
_____ day of _____, 19 ____.

(Signature) _____

Testator name

Attestation and Witnesses

The foregoing instrument was signed, sealed, published, and
declared by the said ___*(name)*___ as his Last Will and Testament, in the presence of each of us, who at his request and
in his presence and in the presence of one another, subscribe
our names hereto as witnesses on the day of the date hereof;
and we declare at the time of the execution of this instrument
he, to our best knowledge and belief, was of sound and disposing mind and memory and under no constraint.

*(Signature)*_____residing at *(address)*_____
                                *(city, state)*_____
*(Signature)*_____residing at *(address)*_____
                                *(city, state)*_____
*(Signature)*_____residing at *(address)*_____
                                *(city, state)*_____

Self Proof of Will

I, ___*(name)*___, sign my name to this instrument this
___*(day)*___ day of ___*(month)*___, 19 ____, and being first duly
sworn, do hereby declare to the undersigned authority that

I sign it willingly, that I execute it as my free and voluntary act for the purposes therein expressed, and that I am 18 (14, 19, 21, 25) years of age or older, of sound mind, and under no constraint or undue influence.

(Signature) _____
Testator's name

We, _____ *(name)* _____, _____ *(name)* _____, and _____ *(name)* _____, the witnesses, sign our names to this instrument, being first duly sworn, and do hereby declare to the undersigned authority that the testator signs and executes this instrument as his last will and that he signs it willingly, and that he executes it as his free and voluntary act for the purposes therein expressed, and that each of us, in the presence and hearing of the testator, hereby signs this will as witness to the testator's signing, and that to the best of his knowledge the testator is 18 (14, 19, 21, 25) years of age or older, of sound mind, and under no constraint or undue influence.

(Signature) _____
Witness (1)
(Signature) _____
Witness (2)
(Signature) _____
Witness (3)

STATE OF _____
COUNTY OF_____ ss

Subscribed, sworn to and acknowledged before me by *(name)*, the testator, and subscribed and sworn to before me by *(name)*, _____ *(name)* _____, and _____ *(name)* _____, witnesses, this _____ day of _____, 19 ____.

My Commission Expires: *(Signature)* _____

_____   Notary Public
        (date)   *(address)* _____
                              (city, state)

WILL FORM 2: Wife: Entire Estate to Husband If He Survives; Otherwise to Others

LAST WILL AND TESTAMENT
OF
_____(name)_____

I ___(name)___, a resident of ____(city)____, ___(state)___, hereby make and publish this my Last Will and Testament and revoke all prior wills and codicils.

1. Special Instructions: I direct that all my legal debts and funeral expenses be paid as soon as practicable after my death.

2. Disposition: I give my entire estate to my husband _(name)_ if he survives me. If he does not survive me, I give my entire estate (in equal shares) to the following beneficiary or beneficiaries who survive me: _____ _____.

3. Trust for Minors, If Any: The share of any beneficiary who shall be under the age of 18 (21, 25) years shall not be paid to such beneficiary but shall instead be held in trust to apply to his/her use all the income thereof, and also such amounts of the principal, even to the extent of all, as my Trustee deems necessary or suitable for the support, welfare and education of such beneficiary; and, when he/she attains the age of 18 (21, 25) years, to pay him/her the remaining principal, if any. If any beneficiary for whom a share is held in trust should die before having received all the principal thereof, then upon his/her death the remaining principal shall be paid to his/her then living child or children, equally if more than one, and in default thereof, to my then living descendants, per stirpes.

4. Executor: I appoint my husband, ___(name)___, executor hereunder and if he shall fail to qualify, or having qualified shall die, resign, or cease to act as Executrix, then I appoint ___(name)___ to act hereunder. No Executor named herein shall be required to give bond.

5. Guardian: If it shall be necessary to appoint a guardian for any minor child of mine, I appoint ___(name)___ as such guardian. If he shall fail to qualify, or having qualified, shall

die, resign, or cease to act as such guardian, then I appoint ___*(name)*___ to serve as such guardian.

6. Trustee: In the event any trust shall come into existence under this will, I appoint ___*(name)*___ as Trustee hereunder. If he shall fail to qualify, or having qualified, shall die, resign or cease to act for any reason, I appoint ___*(name)*___ to act as such Trustee. No Trustee named herein shall be required to give bond.

7. Simultaneous Death Clause: If any beneficiary and I should die in a common accident or disaster, or if any beneficiary dies within 30 (60, 90) days of my death, then all the provisions of this will shall take effect as if such beneficiary had in fact predeceased me.

IN WITNESS WHEREOF, I have hereunto set my hand this _____ day of _____, 19 ____.

_____
(Signature)
Testatrix name

Attestation and Witnesses

The foregoing instrument was signed, sealed, published, and declared by the said ___*(name)*___ as her Last Will and Testament, in the presence of each of us, who at her request and in her presence and in the presence of one another, subscribe our names hereto as witnesses on the day of the date hereof; and we declare at the time of the execution of this instrument she, to our best knowledge and belief, was of sound and disposing mind and memory and under no constraint.

*(Signature)*_____residing at *(address)*_____
                                 *(city, state)*_____
*(Signature)*_____residing at *(address)*_____
                                 *(city, state)*_____
*(Signature)*_____residing at *(address)*_____
                                 *(city, state)*_____

Self Proof of Will

I, ___*(name)*___, sign my name to this instrument this ____ day of ____, 19 ____, and being first duly sworn, do hereby declare to the undersigned authority that I sign if willingly, that I execute it as my free and voluntary act for the purposes therein expressed, and that I am 18 (14, 19, 21, 25) years of age or older, of sound mind, and under no constraint or undue influence.

(Signature)
_____
Testatrix name

We, _____*(name)*_____, _____*(name)*_____, and _____*(name)*_____, the witnesses, sign our names to this instrument, being first duly sworn, and do hereby declare to the undersigned authority that the testatrix signs and executes this instrument as her last will and that she signs it willingly, and that she executes it as her free and voluntary act for the purposes therein expressed, and that each of us, in the presence and hearing of the testatrix, hereby signs this will as witness to the testatrix's signing, and that to the best of her knowledge the testatrix is 18 (14, 19, 21, 25) years of age or older, of sound mind, and under no constraint or undue influence.

(Signature)
_____
Witness (1)
(Signature)
_____
Witness (2)
(Signature)
_____
Witness (3)

STATE OF _____
COUNTY OF_____ ss

    Subscribed, sworn to and acknowledged before me by *(name)*, the testatrix, and subscribed and sworn to before me by *(name)*, _____*(name)*_____, and _____*(name)*_____, witnesses, this _____ day of _____, 19 ____.

My Commission Expires: *(Signature)*
                                         Notary Public
_____   *(address)*
          (date)   *(city, state)*

WILL FORM 3: Married Person: Residue, After General Bequests, to Surviving Spouse; Otherwise to Issue with Provision for Minors

LAST WILL AND TESTAMENT
OF
_____
(name)

I ____*(name)*____, a resident of ____*(city)*____, ____*(state)*____, hereby do make and publish this will, hereby revoking all other wills by me heretofore made.

1. I direct that all my legal debts and funeral expenses be paid as soon after my death as may be practicable.

2. I give all my personal and household effects and automobiles which I may own at the time of my death, including all insurance policies thereon, to my wife, ____*(name)*____, or, if she does not survive me, to such of my children as survive me, in equal shares, to be determined by my Executrix in her discretion. In case my wife shall predecease me, and any child of mine entitled to a share of the property disposed of by this paragraph shall be a minor at the time of my death, I authorize my Executrix, in her discretion, to retain such share for such minor during minority, or to deliver all or any part of such share in kind to such minor, or to the guardian of the property of such minor, or to the person with whom such minor may reside, or to sell all or any part thereof and to deliver the net proceeds of any such sale to such minor, guardian, or person with whom such minor may reside, in any case without requiring any bond, and to store any part retained and to pay all storage, insurance, and other carrying charges thereof out of any funds held for the benefit of such minor under this will.

3. I give to my *(relationship)*, ____*(name)*____, if he/she survives me, the sum of $50,000.00.

4. I give to the ____*(organization)*____ for its general purposes, the sum of $50,000.00.

5. I give the residue of my estate to my wife, ____*(name)*____, or, if she does not survive me, to my children who survive me, in equal shares.

6. If any principal of my estate shall become distributable to a minor, my Executrix may in her absolute discretion pay over such principal at any time to the guardian of the property of such minor, or retain the same for such minor during minority. In case of such retention, my Executrix may apply such principal and the income therefrom to the support, maintenance, and education of such minor, either directly or by payments to the guardian of the property or person of such minor, or to the person with whom such minor may reside, in any case without requiring any bond; and the receipt of any such person shall be a complete discharge to my Executrix who shall not be bound to see to the application of any such payment. Any unapplied principal and income shall be paid over to such legatee upon his/her attaining majority, or, if he/she shall die before attaining majority, to his/her estate.

7. I constitute and appoint ___*(name)*___, Executrix of this will, and direct that no bond shall be required of any Executrix or Executor.

IN WITNESS WHEREOF, I have signed this my Last Will and Testament this _____ day of _____, 19 ____.

(Signature) _____

Testator's name

(This should be followed by the same attestation, witness and Self Proof of Will as in Will Form 1).

WILL FORM 4: Married Person; Everything to Surviving Spouse Conditioned on Time of Survivorship—Otherwise in Separate Trusts for Children

LAST WILL AND TESTAMENT
OF
(name)

I ___*(name)*___, a resident of ____*(city)*____, ___*(state)*___, hereby revoke my former wills and declare this to be my will.

1. I give, devise, and bequeath all of my estate, of whatever kind and description and wherever situation, to my wife, *(name)*, providing she shall survive me by 30 (60, 90) days.

2. If my wife, ____*(name)*____, shall not survive me by 30 (60, 90) days, then I direct my Executor to divide my residuary estate into two equal parts, and to dispose of the same as follows:

A. Trust for Daughter. I give one of such equal parts to my Trustee, in trust, for the following uses and purposes: to take control and management thereof, and to invest and reinvest the principal and keep the same invested, and to receive the income therefrom, and, after paying the reasonable and proper expenses of the trust, to pay the income therefrom to my daughter, ____*(name)*____, during her life. Upon the death of my daughter, or, if she shall not survive me, then upon my death, my Trustee shall pay over the principal, as it shall then exist, to the issue of my daughter per stirpes; or, if no such issue shall then be living, then to those of my issue who shall then be living per stirpes.

B. Trust for Son. I give the other such equal parts to my Trustee, in trust, for the following uses and purposes: to take control and management thereof, and to invest and reinvest the principal and keep the same invested, and to receive the income therefrom, and, after paying the reasonable and proper expenses of the trust, to pay the income therefrom to my son, ____*(name)*____, until he shall attain the age of 30 (25, 18) years of age, and thereupon to pay over the principal to him as it shall then exist. In the event that my son dies before attaining the age of 30 (25, 18) years, or if he shall not survive me, then upon my death, my Trustee shall pay over the principal, as it shall then exist, to such persons and in such estates, interests, and proportions as my son shall, by his will admitted to probate, appoint; or, in default of such appointment, then to his estate.

3. I appoint my wife, ___*(name)*___, Executrix of this will. If my wife shall fail to qualify or cease to act, I appoint my brother, ___*(name)*___, Trustee of the trusts hereunder. If my brother shall fail to qualify or cease to act in any of the foregoing capacities, I appoint my wife's sister, ___*(name)*___, in such capacity in the place and stead of my brother. I direct that none of these individuals shall be required to file a bond or other security in any jurisdiction for the faithful performance of his/her duties.

In Witness Whereof, I have hereunto set my hand and seal on the _____ day of _____, 19 ____.

(Signature) _____

Testator's name

(Attestation, Witnesses, Self-Proof of Will)

WILL FORM 5: Married Person—One Half in Trust for Spouse; Other Half in Trust for Parents

LAST WILL AND TESTAMENT
OF
(name)

I ___*(name)*___, a resident of ___*(city)*___, ___*(state)*___, hereby make, publish, and declare this to be my Last Will and Testament.

1. I hereby revoke all other wills by me at any time heretofore made.

2. I direct that my debts and my funeral expenses be paid as soon after my death as may be reasonably convenient, and I authorize and empower my Executors, in case any claim is made against my estate, to settle and discharge the same in their absolute discretion.

3. I give and bequeath all my household furnishings, furniture, jewelry, silverware, books, automobiles, wearing apparel, and all other personal effects which may be owned by me at the time of my death, together with all policies of insurance relating thereto, to my wife, ___*(name)*___, if /she survives me.

4. a. I give, devise, and bequeath 50% of the residue of my estate to my Trustees, in trust, to collect and receive the income, and after deducting all expenses incident to the administration thereof, to pay the net income therefrom, in quarter annual installments, as nearly equal as possible, to my wife, ___*(name)*___, during her lifetime. In addition, if in any calendar year, including the year in which my death occurs, the aggregate income of this trust shall be less than *(specific amount)* there shall be paid to my wife out of the corpus of this trust, upon her request within the first three months of the succeeding calendar year, an amount of cash or property sufficient to make the total payments from this trust for such year, including income, equal in value to *(specific amount)*, but if such request is not made for any calendar year, no payments

of corpus shall be made in any subsequent calendar year on account of the amount not so required.

b. I hereby grant to my wife, along and in all events, the power to appoint by her will the entire remaining corpus of the trust, free of this trust, to her estate or in favor of any other person or persons.

c. If my wife predeceases me, or, if having survived me, she has not exercised by her will the power of appointment herein granted to her, I direct that 50% of the residue of my estate, or the remaining corpus of the trust for the benefit of my wife, as the case may be, shall be paid over absolutely to my issue, per stirpes, but, if there be none then living, to my parents, _____(name)_____ and _____(name)_____, equally, or entirely to the survivor of them, or if neither of them be then living, to the persons who would be entitled to inherit the same had I then died intestate owning such property.

5. a. I give, devise, and bequeath the remaining 50% of the residue of my estate to my Trustees, in trust, to collect and receive the income, and after deducting all expenses incident to the administration thereof, to pay the net income therefrom in quarter annual installments to my parents, in equal shares, for their lifetimes, and entirely to the survivor of them for the survivor's lifetime. In addition, if in any calendar year, including the year in which my death occurs, the aggregate income of this trust payable to each of my parents shall be less than _(specific amount)_, there shall be paid to each of my parents, and to the survivor of them, out of the corpus of this trust, upon his or her request within the first three months of the succeeding calendar year, an amount of cash or property sufficient to make the total payments from the trust to each of them, and to the survivor of them, for such year, including income, equal in value to _(specific amount)_, but if such request is not made for any calendar year, no payments of corpus shall be made in any subsequent calendar year on account of the amount not so requested.

b. Upon the death of the survivor of my parents, or at my death, whichever is later, I direct that the 50% of the residue of my estate, or the remaining corpus of the trust for the benefit of my parents, as the case may be, shall be paid over absolutely to my issue, per stirpes, but, if there be none then living, to my wife, ____*(name)*____, or, if she be not then living, to the persons who would be entitled to inherit the same had I then died intestate owning such property.

6. In the event of any emergency, my Trustees may, within their sole discretion, apply any portion of the corpus of any trust to the support and care of the beneficiary or beneficiaries then entitled to the income of such trust.

7. No person dealing with the Executors or Trustees shall be obligated to see to the application of any moneys, securities, or other property paid or delivered to them, or to inquire into the expediency or propriety of any transaction or their authority to enter into and consumate the same upon such terms as they may deem advisable.

8. I hereby appoint my friend, ____*(name)*____, Executor hereunder and if he shall fail to qualify, or having qualified shall die, resign, or cease to act as Executor, then I appoint ____*(name)*____ to act hereunder. No Executor or Executrix named herein shall be required to give bond.

9. I hereby appoint ____*(name)*____ as Trustee hereunder. If he shall fail to qualify, or having qualified, shall die, resign or cease to act for any reason, I appoint ____*(name)*____ to act as such Trustee. No Trustee named herein shall be required to give bond.

IN WITNESS WHEREOF, I have hereunto set my hand and seal this _____ day of _____, 19 ____.

                                    (Signature) _____
                                    Testator's name

(Attestation, Witnesses and Self Proof of Will)

WILL FORM 6: Married Person: Entire Estate to Spouse or Child If Spouse Predeceases Testator

LAST WILL AND TESTAMENT
OF
_____
(name)

I __*(name)*__, of ___*(city)*___, ___*(state)*___, make this my last will, and revoke all prior wills or codicils.

1. I direct that the expenses of my funeral be paid as soon after my death as may be practicable.

2. I give my entire estate fo my wife, ___*(name)*___, if she survives me.

3. If my wife, ___*(name)*___, does not survive me, I give my estate, in equal shares, to my *(number)* children, *(name)*, *(name)*, and *(name)*. The share of any legatee who shall be under the age of 18 (21, 25) years, shall not be paid to such legatee but shall instead be held in trust to apply to his/her use all the income thereof, and also such amounts of the principal, even to the extent of all, as my Trustee deems necessary or suitable for the support, welfare and education of such legatee; and when he/she attains the age of 18 (21, 25) years to pay him/her the remaining principal, if any. If any legatee for whom a share is held in trust should die before having received all the principal thereof, then upon his/her death the remaining principal shall be paid to his/her then living child or children, equally if more than one, and in default thereof, to my then living descendants, per stirpes.

4. In the event that my wife, ___*(name)*___, shall die with me in a common disaster or accident, or under such circumstances as may make it impossible or difficult to determine which of us died first (or within, 30, 60, 90 days after my death), I direct that my wife shall be conclusively deemed not to have survived me (or predeceased me).

5. I appoint my wife, ___*(name)*___, Executrix hereunder and if she shall fail to qualify, or having qualified shall die, resign, or cease to act as Executrix, then I appoint my brother,

_____(name)_____, and the ___(Bank name)___ of _____(city)_____,
_____(state)_____, as Co-Executors hereunder. No
Executrix/Executor named herein shall be required to give
bond.

6. If it shall be necessary to appoint a guardian for any minor
child of mine, I appoint my sister, ____(name)____, as such
guardian. If my sister shall fail to qualify, or having qualified,
shall die, resign, or cease to act as such guardian, then I appoint my ___(relationship)___, ____(name)____, in her place and
stead.

7. In the event any trust shall come into existence under
this will, I appoint my ___(relationship)___, ____(name)____,
Trustee hereunder to serve without bond. If my
___(relationship)___, shall fail to qualify, or having qualified, shall
die, resign or cease to act for any reason, I appoint such person as my ___(relationship)___, ____(name)____, shall designate, by
instrument in writing duly acknowledged, as his substitute
or successor. No Trustee named herein shall be required to
give bond.

                                    (Signature) _____
                                    Testator's name

        (Attestation, Witnesses and Self-Proof of Will)

WILL FORM 7: Married Person: Entire Estate to Spouse with Alternative Gifts to Children If Spouse Predeceases Testator

LAST WILL AND TESTAMENT
OF
(name)

I *(name)*, a resident of *(city)*, County of *(county)*, State of *(state)*, being of full age and sound and disposing mind and memory, hereby make, publish and declare this to be my Last Will and Testament, and I hereby revoke any and all wills by me at any time heretofore made.

FIRST: I direct that all my legal debts and funeral expenses be first paid out of my estate.

SECOND: After the payment of my legal debts and funeral expenses, I give, devise and bequeath all of my estate, real, personal and mixed of every kind and nature whatsoever and wheresoever situated, to my beloved wife/husband, *(name)*, absolutely and in fee simple, and in the event she/he predeceases me, I give, devise and bequeath all of my said estate to my children absolutely and in fee simple, in equal shares, and if any of my children not be living at the time of my death the share of any deceased child shall go to the issue per stirpes, of said deceased child, but if there be no such issue shall be paid to my issue, then living, per stirpes.

THIRD: I hereby nominate and appoint my beloved wife/husband *(name)*, to be the Executrix/Executor of this my Last Will and Testament, and in the event of the death of the said *(name)*, during my lifetime, or her/his incapacity or refusal to act, I nominate and appoint *(name)*, of *(city)*, as Executrix/Executor. I hereby direct that neither *(name)* nor *(name)* shall be required to give any bond as such Executrix or Executor. (Appointment of Guardian and Trustee for minor children, if appropriate.)

IN WITNESS WHEREOF, I hereunto set my hand, and declare the foregoing instrument to be my Last Will and Testament.

Date this _____ day of _____, 19 ____.

(Signature)
_____

Testator's name

(Attestation, Witnesses, and Self Proof of Will)

WILL FORM 8: Married Person: Entire Estate to Spouse with Alternative Gifts in Trust for Minor Children If Spouse Predeceases Testator

LAST WILL AND TESTAMENT
OF
_____(name)_____

I, __(name)__, residing at __(address)__, City of __(city)__, State of __(state)__, being of sound and disposing mind and memory, and considering the uncertainty of this life, do make, publish and declare this to be my Last Will and Testament as follows, hereby revoking all other former wills by me at any time made.

FIRST: After my lawful debts are paid, I give, devise, and bequeath all my property, real, personal, and mixed, to my wife/husband outright, if she/he survives me.

SECOND, If my wife/husband, __(name)__, should predecease me, then I give, devise, and bequeath all my property, real, personal, and mixed, in equal shares, to my children, me surviving, subject, however, to the provisions of paragraph THIRD.

THIRD: If a child taking under the preceding clause is under the age of 21 at the time of my death, then I give, devise, and bequeath the share of each such child to __(name)__, IN TRUST NEVERTHELESS, for the following purposes and under the following terms:

(1) to invest said share according to the law of the State of __(state)__;

(2) to pay the income and principal of said share to such child or for the benefit of such child, in the discretion of said Trustee;

(3) to accumulate the said income in his discretion and to pay the accumulated income to such child or for the benefit of such child, in whole or in part, as said Trustee sees fit;

(4) to pay accumulated income, if any, and the balance of the principal, if any, to such child when he or she reaches the age of 21. If such child dies before reaching the age of 21, then to pay said accumulated income, if any, and the balance of the principal, if any, to his/her estate.

FOURTH: In the event that my wife/husband, ___*(name)*___, and I shall die under such circumstances that there is no sufficient evidence that we died otherwise than simultaneously, then my wife/husband, ___*(name)*___, shall be deemed to have predeceased me.

FIFTH: I hereby appoint my wife/husband, ___*(name)*___, to be Executrix/Executor of this my Last Will and Testament, to serve without bond. If she/he shall predecease me, I appoint ___*(name)*___ to serve as Executrix/Executor without bond. I appoint ___*(name)*___ as trustee of any trusts created hereunder to serve without bond.

IN WITNESS WHEREOF, I have hereunto subscribed my name and affixed my seal this _____day of_____, 19 ____.

                                        (Signature)
                                        Testator's name

(Attestation, Witnesses, and Self Proof of Will)

WILL FORM 9: Married Person: No Children; Entire Estate to Spouse with Alternative Gifts to Brothers and Sisters

LAST WILL AND TESTAMENT
OF
_____(name)_____

I, _(name)_, of the City of __(city)__, County of _(county)_, State of ___(state)___, being over the age of eighteen years, and of sound and disposing mind and memory, do hereby make, publish and declare this to be my Last Will and Testament, and hereby revoke all wills and codicils heretofore made by me at any time.

FIRST: I direct that all my just debts and funeral and testamental expenses be paid as soon after my decease as conveniently may be done.

SECOND, I give and bequeath to ___(name)___ the sum of _____(specific amount)_____ Dollars ($_____).

THIRD: All the rest, residue, and remainder of my estate, real, personal, and mixed, of every kind and nature whatsoever, and wheresoever located, I give and bequeath to my beloved wife/husband, ___(name)___, absolutely and forever.

In the event, however, that my said wife/husband shall predecease me, or shall die simultaneously with me, or so nearly so that it cannot be determined which of us survived the other, then, in any of such events, all of the said residue to which she/he would have been entitled shall be divided into as many equal shares as there are brothers and sisters of mine living at my death and brothers and sisters of mine who have predeceased me leaving issue living at my death. One such share shall be paid over to each brother and sister of mine who is then living, and one such share shall be paid over to the issue, per stirpes, of each brother and sister of mine who has predeceased me leaving issue living at my death.

FOURTH: I hereby nominate, constitute and appoint my wife/husband, ___*(name)*___, to be the Executrix/Executor of this my Last Will and Testament, and in the event of her/his death during my lifetime or her/his incapacity or refusal to act, I nominate, constitute and appoint ___*(name)*___ of _*(city, state)*_, as Executrix/Executor. I hereby direct that neither my said wife/husband, or the said ___*(name)*___ shall be required to give any bond as such Executrix/Executor.

IN WITNESS WHEREOF, I have hereunto set my hand, and declare the foregoing instrument to be my LAST WILL AND TESTAMENT.

Dated this _____day of_____, 19 ____.

(Signature)
_____
Testator's name

(Attestation, Witnesses, and Self Proof of Will)

WILL FORM 10: Widows and Widowers with Children: Entire Estate Outright to Children

LAST WILL AND TESTAMENT
OF
(name)

I ___*(name)*___, declare this to be my will and revoke all former wills and codicils which I have made.

FIRST: All obligations of my estate shall be paid. These shall include all death taxes and deficiencies, interest and penalties thereon, assessed in any way by reason of my death, whether on property passing under my will or otherwise. As to death taxes assessed against my estate on property not passing under my will, I direct my Executor not to seek contribution from the recipient for his/her share of such taxes.

SECOND: I give all of my goods and chattels, including my household furniture and furnishings, automobiles, books, pictures, jewelry, watches, silverware, china, and wearing apparel in equal shares to my children who survive me.

THIRD: All the residue of my estate, real or personal, and wherever situated, including lapsed legacies and any property over which I may have a power of appointment, I give and devise per stirpes to my descendants who survive me.

FOURTH: I appoint ___*(name)*___ Executor/Executrix of this will, and I give him/her the following powers, authorities and discretions, to be exercised if he/she chooses, without order of court:

A. To sell at any time or times, at public or private sale, and to mortgage or lease, all or any part of the property, real or personal, of my estate, on such terms as he/she deems best;

B. To settle claims in favor of or against my estate as he/she deems best;

C. To distribute the residue of my estate passing under Paragraph THIRD to the distributees thereof either in cash or in kind, or partly in each, as he/she deems best;

D. To make, execute and deliver any and all deeds, contracts, mortgages, bills of sale or other instruments necessary or desirable in order to exercise the powers, authorities and discretions granted in subparagraphs A through C.

If for any reason ___*(name)*___ does not act or continue to act as Executor/Executrix, then ___*(name)*___ is appointed Successor Executor/Executrix with all of the powers, authorities and discretions conferred on ___*(name)*___ as Executor/ Executrix hereunder. Neither the Executor/Executrix nor the Successor Executor/Executrix shall be required to post bond for the faithful performance of his/her duties.

FIFTH: I appoint ___*(name)*___ guardian of the estate and of the person of any minor children of mine who survive me.

IN WITNESS WHEREOF, I have signed this will, consisting of ___*(number)*___ typewritten pages, the witnesses' certificate included, and on the margin of each page except this page I have signed my name for greater security, this _____ day of _____, 19 ____.

                                        (Signature)
                                        Testator's name

(Attestation, Witnesses, and Self Proof of Will)

WILL FORM 11: Unmarried Persons

LAST WILL AND TESTAMENT
OF
_____
(name)

I, __*(name)*__, of the city of __*(city)*__, State of __*(state)*__, make this my last will, and revoke all prior wills or codicils.

1. I direct that the expenses of my funeral be paid as soon after my death as may be practicable.

2. I give my entire estate to my mother, __*(name)*__, or, if she predeceases me, then to my father, __*(name)*__, or, if both predecease me, then to my *(relationship)*, __*(name)*__ and __*(name)*__, share and share alike.

3. I appoint my mother, __*(name)*__, Executrix hereunder, and if she shall fail to qualify, or having qualified, shall die, resign, or cease to act as Executrix, then I appoint my father, __*(name)*__, Executor hereunder. No Executrix/Executor shall be required to give bond.

4. If any beneficiary and I shall die in a common accident or disaster or under such circumstances that it is doubtful who died first, then all the provisions of this will shall take effect as if such beneficiary had in fact predeceased me.

IN WITNESS WHEREOF, I have hereunto set my hand this _____ day of _____, 19 ____.

_____
(Signature)
Testator's name

(Attestation, Witnesses, and Self Proof of Will)

WILL FORM 12: Holographic Will (Handwritten)

Last Will of _____*(name)*_____

This is my will, and I revoke all prior wills. I give all my property to my wife/husband, _*(name)*_, if she/he survives me, and if she/he predeceases me, then I give my property to my children, share and share alike.

I appoint my wife/husband, ___*(name)*___, Executrix/ Executor of this will and waive all bonds. This will is written, dated, and signed by me in my own handwriting.

Date this _____ day of _____, 19 ____.

_____*(Testator's Signature)*_____

WILL FORM 13: Codicil

LAST WILL AND TESTAMENT
OF
(name)

WHEREAS I, *(name)*, on *(date)*, 19 ___, signed, sealed, declared and published my Last Will and Testament in the presence of ___ *(name)* ___, ___ *(name)* ___, and ___ *(name)* ___, who signed the said will and testament as witnesses; and

WHEREAS, I am desirous of adding an additional bequest and devise in the said will, I, therefore, make and publish this codicil to said will not in conflict with this codicil.

1. I hereby give, bequeath, and devise to ___ *(name)* ___, my daughter mentioned in my will, my solitaire diamond ring, and ten shares of stock in the ___ *(company name)* ___, to be hers absolutely, without accountability in the distribution provided for in the residuary clause of my said will.

2. In the event ___ *(name)* ___, my said wife/husband, after qualifying as Executrix/Executor marries or departs this life, then and in that event I appoint ___ *(name)* ___, my son, sole executor of my will, in the place of his mother/father, conferring upon him generally the same powers in reference to my said estate as are conferred upon my wife/husband in my said will.

3. The special bequests and devises made to ___ *(name)* ___, my wife/husband in the third paragraph of my original will, I intend and declare to be in lieu of dower/curtesy or statutory share in the event my wife/husband should elect to take under my said will.

IN WITNESS WHEREOF, I have signed and published this will on this _____ day of _____, 19 ___.

(Signature) _____
Testator's name

(Attestation, Witnesses, and Self Proof of Will)

WILL FORM 14: Revocation of Will

REVOCATION OF
LAST WILL AND TESTAMENT

WHEREAS, I, *(name)*, on *(date)*, 19 ____, signed, declared and published my last will and testament in the presence of ___*(name)*___, ___*(name)*___, and ___*(name)*___, who signed the said will and testament as witnesses; and

WHEREAS, I am desirous of revoking said will and testament, I do, therefore, hereby revoke said will and testament (or any portion which the testator may desire to revoke) and I do hereby declare it to be null and void to the same extent as though I had never signed it.

IN WITNESS WHEREOF I have signed and published this Revocation of Will on this_____day of_____, 19 ____.

                                          (Signature)

                                  Testator's name

(Attestation and Witnesses)

WILL FORM 15: Nuncupative Will (Dictated to Notary in Louisiana)

LAST WILL AND TESTAMENT

Before me, *(name)*, clerk of the *(name)* District Court in and for the Parish of *(parish name)*, duly commissioned and qualified as such, and ex officio notary public, in the presence of *(number)* competent witnesses residing in the Parish of *(parish)*, State of Louisiana, *(testator name)*, a resident of *(city or parish)*, State of Louisiana, personally came and appeared and declared unto me, notary, in the presence of the undersigned witnesses, that he/she wished to make his/her last will and testament and that he/she wished me to receive his/her last will and testament; and he/she, the said testator/testatrix, dictated to me this his/her last will and testament in the presence of the witnesses; and I, notary, received it from his/her dictation and wrote down the same as it was dictated to me in the presence of the said testator/testatrix, and the witnesses, in the following words, to wit:

I, *(name)*, being of sound mind and knowing that life is precarious, wishing to make a proper disposition of my property in the case of my death, in the presence of the undersigned notary and witnesses do make and declare this my last will and testament, revoking all former wills and testaments whatsoever.

1. I desire that all my just debts be paid.
2. I give and bequeath unto my daughter, *(name)*, of *(city, state)*, the sum of *(specific amount)* dollars.
3. I give and bequeath unto my son, *(name)*, of *(city, state)*, the sum of *(specific amount)* dollars.
4. I give and bequeath unto *(name)*, of *(city, state)*, the sum of *(specific amount)* dollars.

5. All the remainder of my property, whether real or personal, which I may leave at the date of my death, I give and bequeath unto my wife/husband, ___*(name)*___, and make and appoint her/him the Executrix/Executor of this my last will and testament, and give her/him all rights to my estate from the moment of my death, and dispense with the necessity of any bonds.

This last will and testament of ___*(name)*___, was dictated by her/him to me, notary, in the presence and hearing of the witnesses, and was reduced to writing by me, notary, as dictated.

I, notary, then read the above will to her/him in the presence of the witnesses, that she/he was entirely satisfied with the will, and she/he signed it in my presence and in the presence of the witnesses, and the whole was received, dictated, read, and signed at one time, without interruption and without turning aside to any other act.

This was done, read, and signed at the residence of the testator, in the Town and Parish of _____*(parish)*_____, State of Louisiana, on this the_____day of_____, 19 ____.

*(Signature)*_____
Testator's name

*(Signature)*_____
Notary Public

(Attestation and Witnesses)

Optional Will Provisions

The following examples are representative of the most commonly used optional provisions appearing in wills. These provisions and adaptations of them, along with the variety of will forms preceeding this section, should cover about 99% of the specific situations one might encounter. If you are in that other 1%, you may wish to consult an attorney.

Executors to Hold Property for Minor Child

If any legatee under this will shall be a minor at the time of my death, I authorize my executors, in their sole and absolute discretion, as they may deem best, either to sell any of the property to which such minor may be entitled under this will, or to hold such property for him or her (without bond) until he or she shall reach the age of 18 (21, 25) years, or until such earlier time as my executors may deem proper to deliver such property to such minor or to such person (without bond) with whom such minor shall reside, for the benefit of such minor.

General Gifts

I give the sum of five thousand dollars ($5,000) to my friend, ____*(name)*____, if he/she survives me.

Specific Gifts

I give to my son, __*(name)*__, and my daughter, __*(name)*__, share and share alike, per stirpes and not per capita, the real property owned by me at *(city, state)*, which land is more particularly described as follows:*(address or information from deed).*

Disinheritance of Heirs Not Named

I have intentionally omitted all my heirs who are not specifically mentioned herein, and I hereby generally and specifically disinherit each, any, and all persons whosoever claiming to be or who may be lawfully determined to be my heirs at law, except as otherwise mentioned in this will.

Omission of Any Person Except Spouse

I have intentionally omitted to mention, or to give anything to any person or persons other than my wife, __*(name)*__.

Bequest to Surviving Children

I give to my children who shall be living at the time of my death my entire estate, equally to be divided between them; and if any dispute should arise with respect to the division, I authorize my Executor to distribute the effects equally among my children.

Division Per Stirpes

I give __*(property description)*__ to *(name)* and *(name)*, their heirs, executors, administrators, and assigns, their descendants to take per stirpes and not per capita.

Division Per Capita

Should any legatee predecease me, leaving children surviving me, such children shall take per capita, share and share alike, and not per stirpes.

Gift of Automobiles and Furniture

I give to my wife, __*(name)*__, all my automobiles and household furniture and effects together with any and all insurance policies thereon.

Gifts of Personal Effects and Household Goods

All my jewelry, clothing, personal effects, books, paintings, works of art, and all household goods and household furnishings of every description I give to __*(name)*__.

Specific Devises

I give, devise, and bequeath to my wife, ___*(name)*___, if she survives me, in fee simple, the buildings and land located at ___*(address)*___, City of ___*(city)*___, State of ___*(state)*___. If my wife does not survive me, this gift shall lapse and the property described herein shall fall into and become part of my residuary estate.

I give and devise to my wife, ___*(name)*___, if she survives me, or if not, in equal shares to my children who survive me, their heirs and assigns forever, all real estate owned by me at the time of my death, including all buildings and improvements thereon, and all rights and other interests pertaining thereto.

I give and devise to my son, ___*(name)*___, and my daughter, ___*(name)*___, share and share alike, per stirpes and not per capita, the real property owned by me at *(city)*, County of ___*(county)*___, State of ___*(state)*___, and further described as follows:
___*(address or information from deed)*___

Specific Legacies

I give and bequeath to my wife, ___*(name)*___, if she survives me, all my furniture, furnishings, books, linens, silver, china, glassware, jewelry, wearing apparel, automobiles, and all other household and personal goods and effects.

To my daughter, ___*(name)*___, I give my diamond ring and my gold watch. If my daughter does not survive me, this legacy shall lapse and become part of my residuary estate.

I give and bequeath all my law books, office equipment, and all property contained in my law office to my son, *(name)*, if he shall survive me.

General Legacies

I give and bequeath the sum of $ ___*(specific amount)*___ to ___*(name)*___ if he/she survives me, or if he/she does not, then per stirpes to those of his/her issue who survive him/her.

I give and bequeath the sum of $ _(specific amount)_ to my friend, ___(name)___, if he/she survives me.

I give and bequeath $ _(specific amount)_ to my sister, _(name)_, of _(city, state)_ payable from any funds I may have on deposit in any type of account in the _(bank or trust name)_.

Testamentary Trust Clauses

All the rest of my estate, including property over which I have a power of appointment, I give, bequeath, devise, and appoint to my trustee in trust for the following purposes:

(1) My trustee shall hold, manage, invest, and reinvest the principal, shall collect the income therefrom and shall pay the net income therefrom to my wife during her life.

(2) My trustee shall pay to my wife from time to time such sums from principal as will in the discretion of my trustee permit her to maintain the standard of living to which she was accustomed during my lifetime. In making such invasions of principal my trustee shall not consider any other resources of my wife or any other sources of income.

(3) Upon the death of my wife or at my death if she should predecease me, my trustee shall pay or distribute the then principal of the trust to and among my issue who are then living in equal shares per stirpes, or if there are no such issue then living, my trustee shall pay or distribute the then principal of the trust to and among those of my nephews and nieces who are then living in equal shares per capita.

If my wife, ___(name)___, survives me, I give to my trustee the sum of $ _(specific amount)_ in trust to pay the net income in semiannual installments to my wife for a period of ten (10) years following my death or until her remarriage or death before then. The trust shall terminate upon the happening of the first of these events to occur and the principal shall be paid over absolutely to my wife if she is then alive and unmarried or otherwise to my issue per stirpes.

I give ___(percent or all)___ of the residue of my estate to my trustees for the following purposes:

(1) The same shall be divided into two (2) equal shares, and one (1) share shall be held in trust for my son, *(name)*, and the other for my daughter, ___*(name)*___.

(2) The income from each share shall be accumulated until the beneficiary thereof has attained the age of ___*(number)*___ ( ) years.

(3) The principal and accumulated income of each share shall be paid to the beneficiary thereof when he or she attains the age of ___*(number)*___ years. Should either of my children predecease or die before reaching age ___*(number)*___, their share shall be added to the share of the survivor. Should both my children predecease me or die before reaching age ___*(number)*___, then one-half (1/2) shall be divided per capita amont those of my nephews and nieces who are living at the death of the survivor of my two (2) children, or at my death, as the case may be.

Spendthrift Trust Clause

The income reserved to the respective beneficiaries of any trust created by this will shall not be subject to anticipation, or to pledge, assignment, sale, or transfers in any manner nor shall any beneficiary have power in any manner to charge or encumber such interest, nor shall such interest be liable or subject in any manner while in the possession of the trustee for the liabilities of any beneficiary, whether such liabilities arise from his debts, contracts, torts, or other engagements of any type.

No principal or income payable, or to become payable, in any trust created by this will shall be subject to anticipation or assignment by any beneficiary thereof, or to attachment by or to the interference or control of any creditor of any such beneficiary, as to be taken or reached by any legal or equitable process in satisfaction of any debt or liability of such beneficiary, prior to its actual receipt by the beneficiary.

I direct that all legacies and devises and all shares and interests in my estate, whether principal or income, while in the hands of my executor or trustees, shall not be anticipated, alienated, or in any other manner assigned or transferred by

the legatee, devisees, or beneficiary, and such interest shall
be for the sole and separate use of the legatees, devisees, and
beneficiaries, and shall be free and exempt from anticipation,
execution, assignment, pledge, attachment, distress for rent,
and other legal or equitable process which may be instituted
by, and on behalf of, any creditor or assignee of such legatee,
devisee, or beneficiary, or his or her spouse.

Abatement and Preference Clauses

If my estate is insufficient to pay all bequests and devises,
I direct that the order of abatement shall be general legacies,
specific legacies, and then specific devises. All bequests and
devises of the same class shall abate proportionately, provided only that abatement of any legacy or devise to my wife shall
not begin until all other bequests and devises in the same class
have been abated completely.

If my estate is insufficient to pay all of the legacies in full,
then I direct that the legacies to my wife shall be first paid
in full.

If my estate is insufficient to pay all of the general legacies
in full, I direct that the general legacies be paid in the con-
secutive order in which they are set forth in this will.

Business Interests

I direct my Executor/Executrix to discontinue and liquidate,
as soon after my death as is practical, any business or business
interests which I may own at my death, upon such terms as
in the discretion of my Executor/Executrix shall be in the best
interests of my estate. In carrying out such liquidation my Ex-
ecutor/Executrix may sell any such business or business interest as a unit or may sell the assets of any such business
separately from time to time, and such sale or sales may be
consummated at public sale or by way of negotiated sales, and
in either case upon such terms of payment and credit as my
Executor/Executrix shall determine.

I authorize my Executor/Executrix to continue any business
which I may own at my death for such period of time as in

the discretion of my Executor/Executrix shall be in the best interests of my estate, without liability for any losses incurred in carrying on such business or for any depreciation in the value of any of the assets thereof. None of the general assets of my estate, however, shall be used or employed directly, or indirectly, in carrying on such business, nor shall these general assets become liable for any debts of such business. My Executor/Executrix may in his/her sole discretion, transfer all or part of the net assets of such business to a corporation organized by him/her in return for all or part of its capital stock, and in such event my Executor/Executrix may hold such corporate stock for such period of time as, in his/her discretion, shall be in the best interests of my estate, and shall have the power during such period to participate directly, or indirectly, in the management of this corporation.

Bequest of Business

I give and bequeath the goodwill and benefit of the business of ___*(company name)*___, which I am now carrying on at ___*(city, state)*___, and also all my capital and property which shall be employed therein at my decease and also the leasehold premises situated at ___*(address)*___, wherein said business is now being carried on, for all my term and interest therein, unto my son, ___*(name)*___, absolutely.

General Bequest of Items of Personal Property

I give and bequeath to ___*(name)*___ all of my household furniture, rugs, paintings, works of art, ornaments, tapestry, silverware, plate, books, linen, china, glassware, and all other household goods and supplies that I own at the time of my death.

Bequest of Expenses for College Education

It is my will and desire that ___*(name)*___ shall have the benefit of four (4) years of college education, and I direct that my trustee pay from my estate all expenses of attendance for four (4) years at a recognized college, said expenses not to exceed the sum of $_____*(specific amount)*_____ dollars.

Bequest of Unpublished Manuscripts

To ___*(name)*___, all unpublished manuscripts, to be handled by her/him in accordance with instructions which I have given.

Bequest of Papers, Letters, and Documents

I give and bequeath to ___*(name)*___ all letters, papers, manuscripts, diaries, and other writings. This bequest, however, does not include legal documents, such as agreements, contracts, deeds, notes, or mortgages.

Devise of Family Home

If I own a house and plot of ground at the time of my death, which is being used by me and my wife as a family home, then I give, devise, and bequeath such house and plot of ground unto my said wife, subject, however, to any encumbrance or encumbrances thereon existing at the time of my death (or free and clear of any encumbrance thereon existing at the time of my death).

PART II

AVOIDING PROBATE

Introduction

Part I explained, with easy-to-follow instructions, how to write your own will, without a lawyer, and with full confidence in its legality. Part II explains what probate is, what is involved in probate proceedings, and how you can avoid it entirely by the use of the Revocable Living Trust and other probate avoidance methods and techniques. Estate planning is no longer a monopoly for lawyers. You can now do it yourself!

Probate is the legal process by which property and property rights are transferred from a decedent to others. From a time "from whence the memory of man runneth not to the contrary" the probate system has been dominated and controlled by lawyers and judges. The probate statutes, laws and procedures have become fossilized, archaic, outdated and out of step with the reality of our modern society.

Because of the antiquated laws, evolved by the judges and legislatures controlled by lawyers, and the resulting high costs of administration, extravagant legal fees, delays, court costs and other expenses, most citizens in this country have become disenchanted with the entire probate process and the mystique that enshrouds it. American citizens have been cast into a cloud of darkness as to how to intelligently plan an estate to avoid the abuses and scandals so frequently reported by the press.

A few years ago Americans became so disgusted with the probate scandals that something had to be done for their survival. Rather than having each generation being subjected to what the average citizen called the *probate rip-off*, where a large percentage of a family estate was taken away, the concept of avoiding probate by placing assets in trusts became an estate planning tool for those who resented the excessive charges, and the occasional embezzlement or outright theft by lawyers and judges. The cases from which these scandals arose were, for the most part, carefully orchestrated probate processes carried on routinely by the people who so completely controlled the probate system that it was very difficult to obtain any legal recourse. Moreover, an occasional impeachment of a probate judge or the disbarment of a crooked lawyer did not always result in the people getting their stolen money back. Even in those cases where some restitution was made, the legal fees for litigation would take away most of the recovery.

There are several good plans for avoiding probate, and each will be discussed. However, the plan that is so simple, easy and inexpensive — the one that lawyers do not seem to like — is the Revocable Living Trust.

In the beginning the purposes of probate laws were to determine the validity of a will and to protect the estate until it could be distributed according to the directions of the testator or the applicable statutes. In the early days when estates normally consisted of land, and all the interested parties and the property were usually located in the same area, it is easy to see how each state had its own set of probate laws, frequently different from other states. There was little need in those days for uniformity. However, in modern times estates are often composed of paper assets — stocks, bonds, pension plans, insurance benefits, and vacation homes or condominiums in far off places. People are more mobile now, with potential heirs living in many different places.

The old probate laws are simply outdated, unrealistic, burdened with complexity, and administered by lawyers and judges who seem to be preoccupied with obfuscation and habit.

The Uniform Probate Code has made some progress in simplifying the procedures, but much remains to be done. The Uniform Probate Code eliminates the need for a lengthy and complicated settlement process when a will is not contested. This reduces legal fees, court costs and delays. The Code clarifies the status of *will substitutes*, such as jointly held property and bank accounts, and establishes a reasonable distribution of assets, mostly to the surviving spouse or other close family memebers, when there is no will.

The Uniform Probate Code has been adopted in part in only a few states at this writing over the vociferous objections of those individuals and organizations having vested interests in the old process.

The inefficiency of the probate system, the conspiracy of silence among the members of the legal community, the inability of the judicial system to make any significant improvements, and the frustration of the public has resulted in an avalanche of probate avoidance methods and techniques. The legal community, of course, continues to resist the concept that laymen can handle legal problems themselves. However, during the past few years there has been an exciting boom in the scramble to avoid probate. Along with this awareness of the public that they can avoid probate without the services of a lawyer has come the publication of a variety of legal guides and kits designed to tell people about these plans—and demonstrate how to use them, legally.

These methods are easy to understand, and very easy for laymen to use. It is simply a matter of getting accurate information and instructions.

The Revocable Living Trust, the most popular method for avoiding probate, is as easy to prepare as your own will. The Revocable Living Trust involves an agreement by which one party, the grantor, transfers property to a trustee to hold for

the benefit of another, the beneficiary, and is created during
the lifetime of the grantor, the person creating the trust.

Revocable means that the grantor retains the right to
revoke the trust, change its terms, or regain possession of the
trust property. An irrevocable living trust exists when the
grantor relinquishes title to property placed in the trust and
gives up all right to revoke, amend, alter, or terminate the
trust.

One person can be grantor, trustee and beneficiary. This
principle of law is the basis upon which many people avoid
all probate processes. Typically, a person can create a
revocable trust in which he is co-trustee with another person,
for example, an adult child or partner, to hold and manage the
estate, and upon the death of the grantor there is no probate
of the trust property. It is that simple.

This is an easy procedure, used by many people, which you
can employ to completely avoid probate and still have complete control over all of your property. Here are the steps in
the procedure:

- You execute a revocable living trust agreement in which
  you are co-trustee with another person.
- You can convey all, or any part, of your property.
- You provide for income for yourself during your lifetime.
- You provide that upon your death the property is to be
  distributed by the co-trustee as you direct in the trust
  agreement.

The main characteristics of this kind of arrangement are:

- You can cancel at any time during your life.
- You retain complete control of your assets.
- You can receive all benefits and income.
- There is no probate, no probate expenses, confusion, in-
  timidation or humiliation.
- Your beneficiaries can get their inheritance immediately.
- There are no public proceedings nor court records; your
  financial affairs are kept private and confidential.

Probate

When a person dies, he is no longer able to exercise dominion or control over the property he owned or controlled during his life. Through proper estate planning prior to death a person may direct and articulate with particularity what shall and shall not be done with his property.

If a person wants to dispose of property by will, as permitted under the law, the property must pass according to the terms of a valid will. If, on the other hand, a person does not have a will, the law, as set out in the statutes of each state, through the laws of descent and distribution, or intestate succession, provides for the transfer of the property to the persons designated in the statutes.

In either event—by will or by statutory law—the passing of property is accomplished by a court drama called probate proceedings, or the probate process.

Probate is a court procedure by which a will is proved to be valid or invalid. This generally includes all matters and proceedings under the probate statutes pertaining to the administration of estates, guardianships, and other personal and estate matters. These proceedings involve the appointment or designation of an executor, personal representative, or administrator, who under the supervision of the probate court, collects, manages, maintains, and distributes the assets of an estate after payment of claims, costs, court fees, and other probate expenses.

Our probate laws were originally formulated in England at a time in which there was very little mobility by most people and in which estates were largely composed of land or pro-

perty affixed to land. The development of our probate laws
in early American history also evolved at a time in which there
was relatively little mobility in our society. However, in
modern times, with a highly mobile society in which families
typically reside in many different states, own various kinds
of property in different states, and are frequently traveling
to numerous locations, the probate laws have become out of
touch with contemporary reality. They represent little more
than an obstacle that must be overcome before an estate can
be settled.

The probate process as it is practiced in America is a vir-
tual cancer upon the legal community, and neither the shame
of scandals, corruption, and excessive greed, nor the dictates
of ethics, conscience, common decency, common sense, or duty
to clients can motivate the lawyers and the legislators to im-
prove it.

Unfortunately, modest estates or inheritances get caught
up in the majestic web of the probate process, and these
modest estates are usually much smaller or nonexistent by
the time they escape from the jaws of the probate trap with
its extravagant fees, unending delays, and probate costs.

What Law Governs?

The law of the place from which the executor or personal
representative derives his authority, as its exists at the time
of administration, governs the administration of estates. Thus,
it is important in the preparation of a will or other estate planning program that you look to the laws of the state where a
person lives or is domiciled and where property is located and
will be probated after death.

Although the laws of each state may vary on some items,
the adoption of the Uniform Probate Code has somewhat
simplified the understanding of the probate laws by some
American citizens. In the final analysis, the court that probates
an estate will apply the laws of the state where the court is
located, with rare exceptions.

What Is the Administration of an Estate?

The administration of an estate is the management of the decedent's estate for the purpose of collecting and preserving the assets, paying debts, and making distribution to those entitled to the property. A personal representative is the person who handles the administration of the estate. An executor is a personal representative appointed by a testator in a will. An administrator is a personal representative appointed by the court to act where there is no executor appointed by a will. Executors and administrators are considered to be officers of the court and they have a high fiduciary duty to the estate and to creditors and beneficiaries. Most are required to make an accounting to the court.

While executors are nominated by the decedent, an administrator is appointed by the court, and generally is a surviving spouse, next of kin, a creditor or a person having an interest in the estate, or a friend of the judge.

As a general rule, any person who is capable of writing a will is competent to act as executor or administrator. However, where management and supervision of assets is involved, the person should have experience in business activities. Some persons may be disqualified to serve as executors or administrators; for example, nonresidents (in some states) and judges of the probate court.

Generally, only a person who has an interest in an estate may apply for the administration of the estate. The order of preference here is also surviving spouse, next of kin, creditors or others having claims, or friends of the probate judge.

Personal representatives generally have the duties and responsibilities to:
- Discover assets of the decedent.
- Collect and preserve the assets.
- Maintain custody, control and management of the estate, including the management of a going business, contracts, business transactions, if any, investments, tort claims, real estate, litigation, and the like until the estate is settled.
- Provide for an allowance to surviving spouse and children.

- Pay all claims, estate taxes, probate expenses, and other obligations.
- Distribute the balance to the beneficiaries.
- Make an accounting to the probate court and obtain an order of discharge.

An essential duty of the executor or administrator after appointment is to collect all assets of the decedent in order that they may be identified and administered. Not only is he responsible in this respect as to all the decedent's property he already knows about, but it is also his responsibility to discover the full extent of the decedent's assets. If he has reason to believe that any asset exists or may exist, even though his knowledge of it is incomplete, he is required to make all investigations necessary to learn the truth. One of his first duties, therefore, is to familiarize himself as fully as possible with the decedent's affairs.

All assets placed in a Revocable Living Trust by a decedent will be entirely exempt from this probate scenario.

Nature of Office of Executors and Administrators

Executors and administrators are not public officers within the commonly accepted meaning of that term, although they are regarded as officers of the court, and the positions they hold are frequently referred to as offices. Actually, the position is a trust. They are trustees, and funds of the estate in their hands are trust funds.

The executor represents the testator and it is part of his duty to see that the will of the testator is properly executed. The executor also represents the legatees for whose benefit probate proceedings are held. An administrator represents the heirs of the deceased in whose interest the law provides for the distribution of the estate by an administrator, but the administrator does not represent any particular heir.

A Trustee of a Revocable Living Trust accomplishes the same objective as probate administration, but without any probate court supervision or lawyer fees and court costs.

Purpose of Administration

The administration of estates involves more than merely interpreting wills and decreeing the evolution of property. It involves the collection of assets, particularly personal assets, and using them for the payment of debts, taxes, and costs of administration until all are paid or the assets exhausted. If, after full administration, a balance remains, the payment of the balance to those entitled to it is called distribution. It is most unfortunate, as previously noted, that some estates are exhausted by administration costs, legal fees, and other probate costs.

Necessity of Administration

Theoretically, administration of a decedent's estate is necessary in all cases, because the title to the personal property does not descend to the next of kin, and without administration there would be no legal authority to represent the estate in litigation or collect assets and pay debts, taxes and other costs. However, there are instances in some states where persons entitled to an estate have been permitted to take posession of property without the necessity of administration, when nothing remained for a final disposition of the estate except distribution of the property. In fact, the Uniform Probate Code, as originally drafted, encourages simplicity of distribution where there are no disputes.

Of course, there is no necessity for the administration of an estate where the owner elects to avoid probate by one of the plans discussed in later chapters.

Appointment, Qualifications, and Tenure of Executors and Administrators

A court makes no initial appointment of an executor; its power is generally limited to recognizing and approving or disapproving an appointment made by the testator. A court will generally carry out the intention of the testator by appointing the executor designated by the testator.

The fact that an executor derives his authority primarily from a will serves to distinguish him from an administrator who is appointed by a probate court from a person or class designated by statute and who derives his power solely from his appointment by the court.

Bonds and/or Good Faith Required

Administration bonds are required to protect creditors and next of kin from loss through the default or fraud of the personal representative. The bonds constitute a means of indemnity to the estate; the bond fees are paid out of the estate.

An executor or administrator has a duty to exercise the utmost good faith in all his transactions affecting the estate. He may not advance his own personal interest at the expense of the heirs, and any fraud by the executor or administrator will justify the court in declaring his acts void. This is the law, but in many probate courts the participants sing a different song.

In the performance of his fiduciary duties, an executor or an administrator must exercise the diligence that an ordinarily prudent person would exercise under like circumstances in his own affairs. He is not an insurer or a guarantor, but he must use ordinary care, prudence, skill, and diligence.

A personal representative may be held liable for losses to the estate resulting from his or her failure to exercise the diligence expected of a prudent and cautious person or from a failure to use common skill and ordinary business caution.

Phases of Estate Administration

In many respects a legal representative steps into the shoes of the decedent and takes his place in all matters having to do with the decedent's property rights and financial obligations. Frequently this involves the executor in nonfinancial matters, including personal relations of the decedent or among the beneficiaries—any of the problems and situations that can confront an individual during lifetime. The possible range of these problems is unlimited.

Estate administration may necessitate involvement in any field of human activity. It may involve problems of personalities and all kinds of other human problems. It may open closet doors to expose family secrets that during life the decedent had carefully concealed. It also affords a cross section of life, of business, of law, of economics, of human vanity and nobility.

On the other hand the administration of an estate offers constructive opportunities to minimize taxes and expenses, to preserve assets, and protect and enhance the security of beneficiaries. The responsibility of a legal representative is great, which emphasizes the care that should be taken by a testator in selecting one. An executor and his risks are correspondingly great, and one should not accept the appointment without realizing the potential personal liabilities involved.

The Uniform Probate Code

As previously suggested, the Uniform Probate Code was intended to provide ways in which the time for probate proceedings could be substantially shortened, the procedures simplified, and the legal fees, court costs and expenses lessened. The Code is a very flexible document. In difficult or controversial estates, it permits all of the formalities which the laws of most states afford. However, in routine, noncontroversial estates, it provides a process for speedy handling and relatively inexpensive settlement and distribution of an estate. There are also avenues which permit lawyers and personal representatives to adopt a middle ground—by taking great precaution in certain matters, but opting for simplicity and speed in others.

The objectives of the system are to provide necessary opportunities and safeguards to permit persons interested in decedents' estates to be able to settle estates with quite minimal contact with the public office. It is inherent in the approach, however, that interested persons, including personal representatives, are enabled to use the court system for binding all interested persons by order following a mailed notice and a hearing. They can secure a final order on any matter which may involve an estate or a personal representative. The key concept is that the court or registrar does not exercise supervisory jurisdiction over its appointees. The court has no authority to check the work of a personal representative or to make orders relating to him, except when either the representative or other interested persons petition for some order or relief in proceedings begun after the appointment has been completed.

Informal Proceedings

Informal proceedings are defined in the Code as those conducted without notice to interested persons by an officer of the court acting as a registrar or judge for probate of a will or appointment of a personal representative.

Under the Code if a decedent leaves a valid will it may be informally probated without the appointment of an executor or other personal representative. Assuming no survivor initiates a formal testacy proceeding, those interested in a decedent's will, or as heirs of a person with no will, may take advantage of the informal proceedings without a formal adjudication process.

Priority for Appointment as Personal Representative

Persons who are not disqualified have priority for appointment as personal representatives in the following order:

- The person with priority as determined by a probated will including a person nominated by a power conferred in a will.
- The surviving spouse of a decedent who is a devisee of the decedent.
- Other devisees of the decedent.
- The surviving spouse of the decedent (without being specified as a devisee).
- Other heirs of the decedent.
- Any creditor 45 days after the death of the decedent.

Application for Informal Probate Proceedings

Under the Code an informal probate or appointment proceeding is initiated by filing an application as described in the statutes.

Applications for informal appointment are directed to the registrar or judge, and verified by the applicant to be accurate and complete to the best of his knowledge and belief as to the information required. Most courts have printed forms for your use.

Duties and Responsibilities of Executor, Administrator or Other Person Interested in the Estate of a Decedent

One of the most elusive things about the probate process that most people who have an interest in the probate of estates do not realize is that most of the work involved in the so-called probate of an estate is not legal work. A lawyer is not required to do it. If you can follow the checklist which follows, you can save a great deal of time, money and frustration simply by knowing what is to be done, who should do it, and how to keep control over the activities of your lawyer rather than just turning it all over to the lawyer. It is simply a myth that all probate matters involve legal work that must be done by lawyers.

Everything you do will save on legal fees, and knowing what should and should not be done by lawyers will also result in great savings for the estate. Your understanding of the procedures will enable you to avoid a lot of the unnecessary work that most probate lawyers routinely do to increase their fees.

It is recommended that you review these step-by-step procedures and do your own research to enable you to do your job efficiently, effectively and competently, and require the same from your lawyer.

Before Probate Proceedings

Most, if not all, of the work to be done before the actual probate proceedings can, and should, be done by the executor or

administrator. Lawyers are not normally required and should
not be involved in these preliminaries.

Notice of Decease

Give notice to all banks, savings and loan associations, credit
unions, brokerage accounts, financial institutions, and other
businesses where the decedent has accounts or business relationships. Obtain passbooks, certificates, factual data, and all
other information about the accounts. It may also be appropriate, depending on the family situation, to give notices
to family friends and business associates. Later, if the probate
proceedings are instituted, a formal notice may be required
to be published.

Insurance

Check insurance coverage on all of the decedent's estate,
including property, casualty, and life insurance. It will be
necessary to determine all coverage for the purposes of pro-
tecting assets, changing insurance coverage as appropriate and
in assisting in making claims on life coverage.

It may be appropriate in some situations to change the name
of the insured from the decedent's name to the estate. In other
situations, where title to property passes on to the
beneficiaries, it may be appropriate to wait and transfer the
insurance coverage along with title to the property.

Although life insurance is generally payable directly to the
beneficiaries, it may be appropriate for an executor to assist
the beneficiaries in the settlement of insurance claims. If life
insurance proceeds are a part of the estate for tax purposes,
it may be necessary for an executor to make proper tax
returns.

Mail

Notify the post office and arrange for receipt of decedent's
mail. It is also generally appropriate when you notify friends
and business associates to request that mail be addressed
directly to you instead of the decedent.

Copy of Will, If Any

Make additional copies of the decedent's will, if any, for beneficiaries, taxing authorities, and others who may need it. You will be surprised to learn how many people have some interest or claim in estates and want a copy of the will. You will also be surprised at the number of people who show great surprise at being left out of a will. Of course, one can get a copy of the will from the probate court, but it is much easier, less expensive, much less trouble, and saves time to have extra copies available.

Copies of Death Certificate

Make several copies of the death certificate as it will be needed in many of the transactions in connection with the collection of the property, and the management and distribution of the estate. Extra copies will be needed for social security, insurance claims, bank transactions, and many other items.

Family Conference

Schedule a family conference at which all interested parties may be advised of the facts available and exchange information and ideas about the handling of the estate.

This could be one of the most important single things you will do in the administration of an estate. The more you know about what has to be done and who should do it, the more you will gain the confidence of the beneficiaries, family members, and others who are interested in the estate. This emphasizes the importance of your learning about the probate process before you are thrust into the role of executor or administrator.

There are a number of subjects that should be discussed at these meetings. Discretion is required as to how many meetings to hold, who attends, what is discussed, and what is done. If you handle it in an efficient manner by being prepared with a checklist or agenda of things to be done, and suggestions as to who should do it, you will not only gain the confidence of all those involved, but you can save a lot of potential conflicts and friction among family members.

You should determine in advance of this meeting what topics should be avoided, what can be accomplished, and how it can be accomplished.

One of the most critical things to take care of is the immediate needs of the surviving spouse and close family members.

Burial Arrangements

Social security or veterans benefits are sometimes involved in making burial arrangements. Rarely will an executor be appointed by the court before the funeral. Therefore, it is generally some member of the family that will assist in making burial arrangements, sometimes under great stress and intimidation. Proper estate planning by the decedent can greatly facilitate what can otherwise be a very complex and expensive ordeal.

Consider Employment of Attorney

The family conference is a good time to discuss the need for the employment of an attorney, and, if so, who. Where a decedent has a regular attorney who assisted in the estate planning, the choice may be easy. However, in a vast majority of the cases, the decedent not only did not have an attorney, but most likely did not have any significant estate plans or other activities calculated to make the administration of the estate any easier.

Thus, you may have to delay a decision as to whether a lawyer is needed. Don't make the mistake that many people make by automatically assuming that a lawyer is required. You must first learn enough about the estate to determine the need for a lawyer.

I have seen many situations where a surviving family would go to an attorney and hire him to probate an estate only to learn later that probate was unnecessary. This is not only expensive and awkward — it can be embarrassing for the attorney and for those who hire him. However, if there are any assets, most lawyers will plunge right in whether they are needed or not.

Safe Deposit Boxes, If Any

List the contents of any safety deposit boxes in decedent's name. Usually most state laws provide that certain persons must be present, including tax authorities, and that an inventory be made of all contents of safety deposit boxes. If you have a box in the joint name of yourself and another person it may not be necessary for the joint owner to have tax authorities hovering around when the box is opened, though some states now require that.

You should then take possession of all valuables and make sure they are properly protected and distributed.

Preliminary Estimate of Estate Property

Make a preliminary estimate of decedent's estate to determine what form the probate and administration of the estate will require. This is the point at which it may first become evident that the estate is so small as to come within the "no probate" provisions of the statutes. This is one of the items you will have researched as soon as you get a copy of your state statute.

Collection and Protection of Property

Search the household, make an inventory of all personal property, and arrange for storage and protection of personal property. Discretion is required where there is a surviving spouse who is living in the home. In fact, you may have very little to do with personal tangible property in this situation. Don't interfere where you are not required by law to do so. Moreover, most decedents and their survivors do not want unnecessary "poking around" by lawyers or executors where they are not necessary.

Real estate protection and management is of particular importance where the decedent owned apartments, business buildings or other real estate that needs day to day management. A going business usually requires immediate attention unless there is a surviving partner or manager.

The title to automobiles in the decedent's name can be especially troublesome. For example, family members will usually want to drive an automobile, but the estate may be liable for any accident in which the automobile is involved. You should make sure all cars have proper insurance coverage and either sell the cars for cash or transfer the title to beneficiaries as soon as possible.

The decedent's checkbooks and bank records may be the greatest source of information about the financial transactions in which the decedent was involved. Moreover, they will be essential for later use in preparing tax returns.

All cash owned by decedent should be accounted for, put to work, used for estate obligations or distributed to the persons who are entitled to receive it.

If the living facilities of a decedent should become vacant it is essential to avoid losses and damages by failure to properly protect and manage the property. Where business property is not being managed by a surviving spouse or partner, it is important to take quick action in disposing of the property or obtaining competent management. Make sure there is adequate insurance coverage on all property.

Transfer title, if appropriate, to personal property. If the estate is uncomplicated, and the probate is not delayed, you will probably wish to transfer title to most personal property directly to the beneficiaries. However, if you anticipate delays, complex or extended litigation, tax claims, or other conflicts that will require long probate processes, you may wish to transfer title to income producing property to the estate. This is a matter of discretion and will depend on the facts in each case. In all events you should be alert to the problems involved and be prepared to solve them without unnecessary confusion or delay.

Collect any rents, interest, dividends, royalties, or debts due to the estate. Until you can complete the administration of an estate it will be your duty to take care of all financial transactions involving the assets of the estate. You may be required to institute legal action to collect some of the debts owed to the decedent or to the estate.

Assemble data on all property owned by the decedent that will not be a part of the probate estate. Jointly owned property, trust property, life insurance proceeds, and other assets may be a part of the taxable estate — for tax purposes only — but pass directly to others without any probate proceedings. Where tax problems occur it will be part of your duty to make tax returns revealing all the facts, including the value and aggregate amounts.

In appropriate cases it may be necessary to have appraisers appointed in the sale or disposition of some of the assets. Don't assume all appraisers are competent or honest. You should carefully review the qualifications of any appraiser appointed, and be sure you have a fee arrangement in writing. Moreover, you may want to take a look at old probate files and be sure you do not hire an appraiser who is a "buddy" of the probate judge and the probate lawyers.

Utilities, Charge Accounts, and Credit Cards

There are a number of business activities of a decedent that should be closed down as soon as possible. Credit cards, unless being used by the surviving spouse or jointly held by descendant or next of kin, should be collected and cancelled. You may want to transfer some accounts into the name of the estate, for example, utilities, telephone, and other services that are needed by you, the family, or business. Otherwise it is appropriate to close out the accounts of a decedent or have them transferred to the surviving spouse or other family members.

Employer Benefits

Many of the decedent's personal matters may be handled by the surviving spouse or other family members. However, it is usually appropriate and proper for an executor to assist in the matters of salary, bonuses, and any distributions from pension or profit sharing plans.

Open Estate Bank Accounts

If the probate is complicated, or, for other reasons, may last a long time, you will probably need a bank account in the name of the estate. This will facilitate your being able to carry on the financial transactions necessary to bring the estate to a close. Generally this will not occur until after probate proceedings are filed and you are officially appointed.

Personal Records and Tax Returns

You should assemble all personal records and tax returns of the decedent so as to bring yourself current on all the financial transactions of the decedent. These records will be essential for obtaining the background information and facts you will need to handle the estate properly, and to prepare tax returns.

Social Security, Civil Service, Veterans, and Other Benefits

These are also items that may be more of a personal problem for the surviving members of the family. However, the filing of required paperwork is frequently handled by an executor. An attorney will charge high fees for this nonlegal work that any layman could do.

Family Allowance and Assistance

Each state statute has a provision for family allowances pending probate of an estate. You can get preliminary information on these items at the first family conference.

Going Business

Obtain all information about any partnership agreements, buy-sell agreements, or other business arrangements of the decedent.

Check any litigation, claims, or other controversies relating to the decedent's property or property interests. In the case of a going business, quick action is needed to manage the business yourself or obtain competent management personnel.

Current Bills and Obligations

You should formulate some estimates early in the probate process as to whether the estate is solvent or potentially insolvent. If you are sure the estate is solvent you may wish to pay current bills and obligations to avoid interest and penalties. However, if questions remain as to whether the estate is solvent, you should be cautious about making any payments on estate obligations. In most situations it may be appropriate to require a claimant to file a claim in the probate proceedings. Telephone and utility bills may have to be paid to avoid termination of services.

Do You Need A Lawyer?

After holding the family conference and completing the preliminary estimate of the estate's assets, you will be in a position to know whether an attorney should be employed to assist in probate court. If no probate is necessary, you can generally forget about hiring a lawyer. Furthermore, in situations where most of the property was jointly owned and there are no tax problems or possibilities of litigation, there is no need for a lawyer. You will be surprised to learn how much you can do yourself by reviewing the statutes and court rules with the intention of doing all of the things you are permitted to do as executor or administrator.

Determining That Probate Is Unnecessary

Your preliminary estimate of assets and your initial review of your state's statutes will enable you to make this determination, usually without the need for a lawyer's advice. In a vast majority of cases a lawyer is not required. Moreover, unless some conflict or controversy arises, there is virtually nothing for a lawyer to do in a small estate—other than doing the executor's work and getting paid legal fees for it.

Probate Proceedings Step By Step

If probate is deemed necessary, due to contesting of the will, estate tax problems, size of the estate, or any other legal reason, you should follow the steps outlined in the following sections.

Preliminary Information

First, determine the domicile of the decedent for probate purposes, the place of administration and the possibility of ancillary probate in other states. Avoid probate in other states when possible. Then determine whether formal or informal probate is appropriate. Keep this question in mind when you first review your state's statutes.

Initial Proceedings In Court

Offer the will for probate or apply for administration. Obtain Letters Testamentary or Letters of Administration and make extra copies of these documents for banks, claims and other transactions. If bonds are required, make arrangements for them. Complete the publication of any notice required by statutes or rules to interested parties and creditors. Arrange for ancillary administration, if necessary. Prepare and file a complete inventory of the decedent's assets with the probate court.

Tax Aspects of Estate Administration

Although you may need an accountant to assist in the preparation of tax returns, you should become familiar with all the necessary forms and the instructions for completing them. These can be obtained from IRS offices. It is recommended that you get a copy of IRS Pubication 559, Federal Tax Guide for Survivors, Executors, and Administrators, and other information on tax requirements for an estate.

Some of the usual requirements that you may have to know about include the following:
- Apply for a tax identification number.
- File Income Tax Return, Form 1040 for decedent.
- File Form 712, Life Insurance Statement.
- File Fiduciary Income Tax Return, Form 1041.
- File Estate Tax Return, Form 706.
- File U.S. Quarterly Gift Tax Return, Form 709.

Claims Against the Estate

Legitimate claims should be paid as soon as reasonably possible to avoid interest and penalties, provided the estate is solvent and has funds available. You should investigate all estate claims to make sure they are valid. In the event litigation should develop, your lawyer can handle it for you, but you can assist by having available all facts, evidence, and witnesses.

Distribution of Estate

Once you are permitted by the court to actually distribute the assets, you should do so in the following order:
- Pay all taxes due.
- Pay all expenses, fees and other administration costs of probate.
- Satisfy all claims against the estate.
- Pay family allowances.
- Satisfy specific bequests.
- Satisfy general bequests.
- Make residuary distribution.

Accounting

Records must be kept of all transactions so you can account to beneficiaries, tax authorities, and the court. You will need a final accounting of all assets for these and other purposes.

Order of Discharge

After completion of all acts necessary to conclude the probate proceedings, file your application for an order of discharge. It is at an end.

The Revocable Living Trust

A trust is a legal relationship in which one person transfers property to a second person for the benefit of a third person. The person creating the trust is called the grantor, trustor, or settler. The person or entity having legal title to the trust property is the trustee, and the person for whose benefit the trust is created is called the beneficiary. The same person can be grantor, trustee, and beneficiary all at the same time in some situations.

The fundamental legal principle you need to understand about a trust is that one person can have two legal entities: as an individual, and as a Trustee. For legal, tax and other purposes a trustee is a separate person or entity from the person as an individual. Therefore, an individual person can transfer property from his or her individual name to himself or herself *as Trustee*, and hold it for himself or herself or for others. Typically, the Revocable Living Trust Agreement provides that title shall be in the name of the trustee or co-trustees and upon the death of the grantor shall go to the designated beneficiary or beneficiaries. When the grantor dies the property is automatically held by the co-trustee or successor trustee for the beneficiaries without any probate process or court proceedings. This may sound like a bit of legal magic, and, indeed, that is exactly what it is: it is an accepted legal fiction to accomplish a noble and worthwhile goal. It avoids probate just as slick as "magic."

Elements of A Trust

The essential elements of a trust are: intention, trust property, trustee, and beneficiary. It is necessary for you to understand the importance of these terms in order for you to create your own trust.

Intention

A trust is created only if the grantor properly expresses an intention to create a trust. Generally, a trust can be created by written instrument, verbally, or by conduct. The Statute of Frauds and Statute of Wills requires that some transactions must be in writing to be enforceable. When the transaction is only oral, the evidence is required to be clear and convincing. No particular form of written wording or conduct is necessary. Even though many oral agreements are legal it is recommended that you always manifest your intentions by a written document, especially in the case of a trust agreement.

Trust Property

A trust cannot be created unless there is trust property that definitely exists. Any transferable interest, present or future, vested or contingent, legal or equitable, in any object of ownership, tangible or intangible, may be held in trust. This would include virtually any kind of property you may own.

Trustee

A trust by its very nature requires that there be a trustee to administer it. However, if you place property in a trust without naming a trustee, or the trustee dies, a court would appoint a trustee to administer the trust. You should be specific in naming a trustee and successor trustees to avoid the unnecessary costs of a court appointment.

As a general rule, any natural person, including the grantor, can hold property in trust in the same way that a person can hold property for his or her own benefit. Moreover, other entities may act as trustees, such as a bank, trust company, or corporation. Where a major objective of a trust is to avoid probate and the excessive fees associated with probate system you may wish to avoid naming an attorney, a bank or trust company because the fees they charge are an integral part of the probate system.

A property owner may declare himself or herself trustee of the property for the benefit of another. In this situation the property owner is both grantor and trustee. The selection of a trustee other than yourself can be one of the most important aspects of creating a trust. Most people select a close family member, friend or relative. Under the typical Revocable Living Trust Agreement the only duty of a successor trustee is to convey the trust property to the beneficiaries. If management of a business or other investments are involved, you may wish to consider a person with business experience.

Beneficiary

A private trust, unlike charitable or honorary trusts, requires a beneficiary with the right to enforce it. The beneficiary must either be specifically named or be reasonably ascertained from facts existing at the time the trust is created.

Any person, natural or corporate, who has the capacity to take and hold title to property may be a beneficiary even though that person may not be capable of administering the property. Indeed, the inability of a beneficiary to manage his or her own property, as in the case of minor children, is often a principal reason for creating a trust.

There may be any number of beneficiaries, and the grantor can be the only beneficiary, or one of several. The trustee may also be a beneficiary with one exception: a sole trustee may not be a sole beneficiary.

Methods of Creating A Trust

You can create a trust:
- by declaring that you hold your property as trustee for yourself and/or others;

- by transferring your property to another person as trustee for yourself and/or others; and

- by transferring, in your will, your property to another person as trustee for others.

Creating a trust by will is called a testamentary trust that must go through the probate system. You should always use a formal written document when creating a trust to avoid any confusion or misunderstanding, and you should not use the testamentary trust if you wish to avoid probate.

Many people have come to consider the revocable living trust as an instrument which incorporates most of the features of a will. It not only accomplishes the objectives of a will more effeciently, less expensively, and in less time, but it has a host of other advantages.

The Revocable Living Trust

The most popular trust, by far, is the revocable living trust. Its use as a technique for avoiding probate has become very popular during the past few years, and it is anticipated that it will continue its dramatic increase in popularity with the general public.

A revocable living trust is an arrangement in which an individual places property in trust, naming himself or herself or some other person as Trustee or Co-Trustee, but reserving the right to revoke the trust so that the property can be returned to the grantor. Generally the trust agreement provides that upon the death of the grantor the property shall go to the named beneficiaries. This automatically avoids all probate of the property. A revocable living trust can also be used to place income producing property in trust to be managed by professional managers. However, the grantor can actively manage the trust property if it is appropriate at any time. The primary purpose is the avoidance of the ineffective, inefficient, cumbersome and expensive probate system.

The use of revocable living trust avoids the delays that are always involved in the probate courts, and prevents disruption that may occur where management of assets shifts after death. A trustee can distribute the assets of the estate immediately after death and needs no lawyers, judges or other legal experts who are preoccupied with make-work paper shuffling to prolong the process. Another advantage is that a revocable living trust preserves the grantor's right of privacy while probate proceedings are a matter of public record.

Advantages of a Revocable Living Trust

In the typical revocable living trust, a grantor transfers property to a trustee under a written agreement. The classic arrangement is for the agreement to provide for the trustee to pay the grantor all of the income from the trust during his or her lifetime, together with such amounts of principal as may be requested by the grantor. It also provides that the grantor can amend or revoke the trust or change the trustee at any time.

Upon the death of the grantor the trust property is held, administered, and distributed by the trustee or successor trustee instead of passing under a will through the probate system. This method is fast, simple, easy, all without the costs and delays of probate. Indeed, it has been said that with a revocable living trust an estate can be completely administered before a lawyer can get to the courthouse to file a will! And it is true. An entire estate can be administered and distributed in a matter of a few hours or days. The express provisions of the trust agreement which apply to the administration and distribution of the trust assets after the death of the grantor become operative and can be carried out immediately.

The revocable living trust is the answer to most of the ugly probate problems. The trustee can perform all of the necessary management of the trust assets, if needed, including the collection of income, the purchase and sale of trust assets, and the management of a closely held business or real estate. In an emergency the trustee can make payment of hospital, nursing and doctor bills, and any other expenses of the grantor. The trust can be revoked by the grantor if he or she so desires, or the grantor may actively manage the trust property while leaving the legal title in the name of the trustee. If the grantor dies, the trust property can be immediately transferred to the designated beneficiaries. To summarize, the advantages of the revocable living trust include the following:

- Avoidance of probate.
- Avoidance of probate administration fees and expenses.
- Avoidance of excessive legal fees for probate.
- Avoidance of unnecessary delays.
- Avoiding publicity of probate matters.
- Avoiding ancillary administration.
- Avoiding statutory restrictions on bequests of property.
- Avoiding inheritance taxes.
- Avoiding will contests.
- Tax savings in some situations.
- Property management.
- Management uninterrupted by incapacity of grantor.
- Assurance of uninterrupted income and access to principal for family beneficiaries.
- Avoiding the emotional trauma, aggravation and frustration of a complicated probate process that does not serve any noble purpose.

Trusts and Taxes

As a general rule, a trust, like an individual, is a taxable entity. A trustee must file an income tax return for the trust and pay the tax on its taxable income unless income is passed through to the beneficiaries — which is usually the case. Many times a trust is established primarily because the beneficiary is in a lower tax bracket than the grantor. The establishment of several trusts can result in income tax savings on a grand scale in some circumstances. Although trusts can avoid probate they do not avoid estate or gift taxes as a general rule. Other techniques are recomended for avoiding estate and gift taxes.

Marital Property Rights

In most states the laws give certain legal rights to a surviving spouse which cannot be defeated by will. Some of these state laws, but not all, also give certain rights to a surviving spouse which cannot be defeated by gifts, by the revocable living trust or other transfers. These marital property rights are called community property, dower, curtesy, elective rights, statutory rights or various other terms. These rights typically gives one-half or one-third, or some other portion of the estate of the decedent to the surviving spouse.

If community property is to be placed in a revocable trust by a married person, the grantor's spouse should join in the execution of the trust agreement. In general community property consists of whatever property is gained during the marriage by the toil, talent or other productive faculty of either spouse. In general property obtained by one spouse by gift, devise or descent is not included in community property. In community property states, you should check the specific laws of your state on this question. The community property states are Arizona, California, Idaho, Louisiana, New Mexico, Nevada, Texas and Washington. Some of the other states also give certain marital property rights to spouses, and these vary from state to state. Therefore, it is suggested that all transfers of property by a married person be signed by the spouse of the grantor. This is not a problem for most married people as they generally own property in joint names.

The concept behind these laws is that with certain exceptions, property acquired during marriage belongs to both spouses. The marital property rights vary from state to state and the state laws with respect to marital property rights transferred by a living trust agreement are inconsistent and sometimes difficult to interpret. It is recommended that any married person obtain the consent of the spouse in any trust created during marriage.

The trust doctrine was not fashioned by the courts as an instrument for denying rights of a spouse. On the contrary, the trust can be used by both married and unmarried persons as an easy, simple, inexpensive way to transfer property from one generation to another without the probate process.

Examples of How The Revocable Living Trust Works

Suppose that a married couple provides in a Revocable Living Trust Agreement that all, or a part of, their assets are declared to be held by them, as Co-Trustees, for their benefit during their lifetimes, and upon the death of either spouse to go to the surviving spouse, or in the event of simultaneous deaths to go directly to designated beneficiaries. Immediately upon the death of either spouse, all legal interests in all the property would automatically revert to the surviving spouse, as sole trustee, free and clear from any probate processes or other court delays. Upon the death of the surviving spouse the property would go to the successor trustee for the designated beneficiaries, free and clear from any probate processes or other court delays. The surviving spouse would have the option to place the assets in another Revocable Living Trust with an adult child or other family member as Co-Trustee and avoid probate again and again.

Suppose further, as a second example, that an unmarried person provides in a Revocable Living Trust Agreement that all, or a part of, his or her assets are declared to be held by the grantor and a third party, as Co-Trustees, for the grantor's benefit during his or her lifetime, and upon the death of the grantor to go to the beneficiaries designated in the agreement. Immediately upon the grantor's death, all legal interest in all the property would automatically revert to the Co-Trustee, as the sole trustee, to be transferred as directed by the grantor in the agreement. If the beneficiary is an adult he or she could be the Co-Trustee and upon the grantor's death he or she would automatically have title to the property for himself or herself.

Trusts Take Precedence Over A Will!

We have been discussing the two principle ways for you to pass your property upon your death to the persons you want to have it either by will or by a trust. The transfer by will requires the probate process; a Revocable Living Trust completely avoids probate.

What happens if you do both—leave property to a person in your will and also leave the same property to another person in a Revocable Living Trust? The Trust takes precedence over the will. For example, if you have $100,000 in stocks and first write a valid will leaving the specific stocks to John Doe, and then later execute a Revocable Living Trust leaving the same stocks to Jane Doe, Jane Doe receives the stocks upon your death because the trust takes precedence. Suppose further that you first placed the stocks in a Revocable Living Trust for John Doe and later executed a valid will leaving the same stocks to Jane Doe. In this case, John Doe receives the stocks. The trust takes precedence over the will no matter whether it was executed before or after the will.

The Revocable Living Trust takes precedence over the will in both cases because the title (ownership) of the property was transferred in each transaction when the trust agreement was executed. The title (ownership) to the stocks could not be transferred by will until the death of the owner. Even though you can revoke a trust and you can revoke a will the trust actually transfers title to the trustee at the time of the execution of the trust and a will does not.

Transferring Title to Property

In transferring title to property from a grantor to a trustee, the execution of the Trust Agreement and listing of the property in the Exhibit "A" schedule of Property is legally sufficient for most property. However, there are various laws and regulations controlling the keeping of records for transfer of some property, and these should be followed to assure that your records are accurate and complete.

Records and Recording Laws

A public record is defined as one required by law to be kept, or necessary to be kept, in the discharge of a duty imposed by law, or directed by law to serve as a memorial and evidence of something written, said, or done. A public record is one made by a public officer in pursuance of a duty, the immediate pur-

pose of which is to disseminate information to the public or
to serve as a memorial of official transactions for public
reference.

The system of recording is regulated by statute in each
state. The recording requirements may vary from state to
state. However, every state has a statutory requirement for
recording of conveyances or transfers of real estate. These
records are usually kept at a county seat by a clerk or recorder.
The typical statute requires the recording of all conveyances
of real property, deeds, mortgages, deeds of trust or instruments in the nature of mortgages, and may include long
term leases, chattel mortgages, mining claims, conveyances
on execution, and other matters affecting real property.

The term *conveyance* has been defined as some written
paper or instrument signed and delivered by one person to
another, transferring the title to or creating a lien on property, or giving a right to a debt or duty.

Real Property

If any real property is included in the list of property in Exhibit "A", you should have the Trust Agreement acknowledged. It is also necessary to have a separate deed executed,
transferring the property to the name of the trustee and then
have the deed and the Trust Agreement recorded in the country where the real property is located. This is to comply with
the recording statutes of the state. You should obtain a real
estate deed in your own state as they vary from state to state.
These documents are available at local real estate offices, law
offices, stationery stores and other convenient places. Since
you must record the real property trust, you may want to have
separate trusts, one for real property, and another for all other
property. This will enable you to record only the real property trust and keep the other matters private in a separate document. Moreover, it is not necessary or appropriate to record
a trust with personal property as trust property.

Personal Property

Stocks, bonds, mutual funds, bank accounts, saving and loan accounts and other similar types of accounts can be included in your trust agreement. However, you need to check with the bank or other financial institution involved to make appropriate changes in their records and certificates of title, if any.

Automobiles, motorcycles, trailers and similar kinds of property generally have a certificate of title that is recorded with the appropriate governmental agency.

The trustee's name is generally entered on these documents as, for example: "John Doe, as Trustee under Revocable Living Trust Agreement dated June 1, 1984." It is frequently abbreviated as follows: "John Doe, as Trustee u/t/d June 1, 1984."

Some of the financial institutions, especially banks, may want a copy of the Trust Agreement in their files. You should check with these institutions and give them directions to make sure your trust agreements will be recognized.

In the event you have occasion to transfer additional property to the trust after it has been established or withdraw assets from it you simply add the new property to Exhibit "A" and date and sign it or delete property and date and sign it. Remember, you reserved the right in the instrument to amend or revoke it at any time.

If any property is jointly owned both owners will, of course, have to sign the Trust Agreement as grantors and also execute any deed or certificate of title.

Selection of Trustees and Successor Trustees

For purposes of avoiding probate, it is generally recommended that the grantor act as trustee or co-trustee. The grantor should consider a co-trustee especially if an adult beneficiary (for example, spouse or adult child) is a primary or sole beneficiary. A grantor who wants a third party trustee should consider adult children, other relatives or business associates. Having a lawyer, trust officer, bank or trust company as trustee defeats one of the major objectives of the trust:

avoiding excessive fees and expenses of probate. It is also very important to appoint successor trustees as this avoids the expenses, delays and inconvenience of court appointments.

Revocation and Amendment

The great advantage of the Revocable Living Trust is your ability, at any time, for any reason, or for no reason, to change it or revoke it. You can do this by the mere stroke of your pen. By using the revocation form you simply describe the trust agreement you wish to revoke and sign the revocation. If the trust agreement is recorded you need to record the revocation. Immediately upon your signing the revocation and transmitting it to the trustee, the trust is automatically terminated and revoked as a matter of law. No lawyers, no judges, or lengthy court proceedings are needed. You are in complete control of your property and it can remain a private matter, since you can keep it out of the hands of the probate lawyers.

This is necessarily a brief treatment of trusts, but the information given here and the forms that follow are entirely adequate for you to avoid probate. You have an absolute right to use a trust and to avoid probate and it is absolutely legal and valid in all states.

Revocable Living Trust Agreement Forms

The essence of avoiding probate via the Revocable Living Trust is simply to transfer title to property to a trustee by a written document. You, the grantor, can maintain complete control, management and authority over the property. You can revoke at any time if you wish. In other words, the only difference is that you, or another, holds the *legal title* to the property, as Trustee, and in the event of death the title to the property automatically — as a matter of law — is held as directed in the trust agreement to be used, or transferred, to the beneficiary or beneficiaries you have designated in the agreement. Thus, the probate of the assets, or transfer through the probate system, is avoided.

The Revocable Living Trust Agreement need not be complicated, complex or mysterious. Each of the provisions of the typical trust are discussed here to demonstrate how simple it is and how you can do it yourself.

Whereas Clause

After preparing the introductory clause which merely states the names and identities of the grantor or grantors and the trustee or trustees, the so-called *Whereas Clause* simply states the grantor's intent, which is an essential element of a trust. It identifies the property and states the purpose of the agreement, the use and disposition of the property.

Transfer of Property

The transfer, or conveyance, of the property is the key to avoiding probate. Since the property is transferred to a trustee the grantor does not own it as a part of his estate to be disposed of in a will.

Disposition of Income and Principal

You have a legal right to direct exactly what is to happen with the property during your lifetime, and after death. You can direct that all such property and all income therefrom shall be used by you or anyone else you designate. In the event any beneficiary is a minor you can direct the trustee to hold the property until the minor reaches majority.

Revocation and Amendment

You have a legal right to cancel the agreement at any time or change it in any way you desire.

Successor Trustee

It is important to have a trustee, a co-trustee, or successor trustee, to hold the title after the death of the grantor. This avoids the necessity for a court appointment—a potentially expensive venture into the domain of the probate system.

Trustee's Acceptance

Since this is an agreement, the other party, the trustee, must agree to the terms of the agreement and sign it.

Signatures

All grantors and all trustees must sign the agreement. Review the discussion about recording the documents in the event of real estate requirements for recording conveyance documents so you can be assured that the transfer meets all the legal requirements of your state's recording laws.

Exhibit "A" Schedule of Property

This is the place for listing and specifically identifying the property that is the subject of the trust. Make sure you use the legal description of real estate to avoid any doubts about the transfer of title on the record.

There are other provisions you can use in the agreements, but these are the essential parts for avoiding probate.

If you have any difficulty in completing the Trust Agreements, you may want to obtain a do it yourself kit with fill in forms. Whether you prepare your own forms from the following samples or use a kit, the following information will assist you in correctly filling in the blanks.

Notes On Using The Forms

Form 16 is for use by a married couple only while the other forms are suitable for any adult. Married persons should consider carefully the marital rights of surviving spouses.

In each form the introductory paragraph should be filled in by listing the complete names and addresses of the grantor or grantors, and the trustee or co-trustees. The following example illustrates this first paragraph.

"This Revocable Living Trust Agreement is made this 15th day of June, 1985, between John J. Doe, and Jane J. Doe, husband and wife, of 123 Main Street, Boulder, Colorado, 80301, herein referred to as Grantors, and John J. Doe and Jane J. Doe, of 123 Main Street, Boulder, Colorado, 80301, herein referred to as co-trustees."

Paragraph 2 provides that the trust estate and income shall be used by the grantor or grantors during their lives, and upon the death of the grantor or grantors the property shall go to the beneficiary or beneficiaries designated in paragraph 2. Make sure you give a sufficient identification of each beneficiary. Keep in mind that you can change or revoke these designations, in writing, at any time.

In paragraph 4 fill in the name of the successor trustee. If he/she cannot serve, you can merely designate another successor trustee, or permit, as provided in paragraph 4, the first designated beneficiary to become trustee.

In paragraph 5 fill in the state of your domicile unless you wish some other state laws to govern.

The document should be fully executed by all grantors and all trustees, have two witnesses sign at the appropriate places and have the document acknowledged. Witnesses and acknowledgment are not legally required in most trusts for personal property under most circumstances. However, it is recommended that the agreement be acknowledged and witnessed as a matter of good practice and for formality. A conveyance of real estate does require acknowledgment and witnesses. Therefore, if real estate is listed in Exhibit A you must have the agreement, and the separate real estate deed, acknowledged, witnessed and recorded. If you have any difficulties with real estate transactions you may wish to have an attorney or a real estate expert assist in the execution and recording of the appropriate documents at the appropriate office.

In Exhibit "A" you should list in detail all property you wish to be included in the trust estate. If real estate is included it should be described with the legal description on the conveyance document (the deed or conveyance documents by

which the grantor received the title to the property) and the
trust agreement should be recorded along with the conveyance
deeds.

You can complete the form agreements for personal property by merely listing all the property in Exhibit "A". Although
the execution and recording of the separate real estate conveyance documents are considered by some to be cumbersome,
it is far less difficult and much less expensive than probate
of the estate.

The primary purpose of the Revocation, Form 20, is to notify
the trustee and to record it in the event the Revocable Living Trust Agreement was recorded. Fill in the appropriate
blanks and make sure it is delivered to the trustee and recorded, if appropriate.

Form 16: Revocable Living Trust Agreement: Husband and Wife: Grantors, as Co-Trustees, For Lifetime Use of Grantors, Then to Others

REVOCABLE LIVING TRUST AGREEMENT

This Revocable Living Trust Agreement is made this ____(day)____ day of ___(month)___, 19 __(year)__, between ____(name)____ and ___(name)___, husband and wife, of _(address)_, City of __(city)__, State of __(state)__, herein referred to as Grantors, and __(name)__ and __(name)__, of _(address)_, City of __(city)__, State of __(state)__, herein referred to as co-trustees.

Whereas, grantors are now the owners of the property described in Exhibit A attached hereto and made a part hereof, and

Whereas, grantors desire to make provision for the care and management of such property, and the collection of the income therefrom, and the disposition of both such income and such property in the manner herein provided:

Now, therefore, for the reasons set forth above, and in consideration of the mutual covenants set forth herein, grantors and trustees agree as follows:

1. *Transfer of Property:* Grantors, in consideration of the acceptance by co-trustees of the trust herein created, hereby convey, transfer, assign, and deliver to co-trustees, their successors in trust and assigns, the property described in Exhibit A attached hereto and made a part hereof, by this reference, which property, together with all other property that may from time to time be held by co-trustees hereunder, is herein referred to as Trust Estate. Grantors, and any other persons shall have the right at any time to add property acceptable to trustees to this trust and such property, when received and accepted by trustees, shall become a part of the trust estate.

2. *Disposition of Income and Principal:* Trustees shall care for and manage the trust estate and collect the income derived therefrom, and, after the payment of all taxes and assessments thereon and all charges incident to the management thereof,

dispose of the net income therefrom and corpus thereof, as follows:

During the lifetime of grantors the trustees may pay income of the trust estate and such portions of the principal as the grantors from time to time may direct to the grantors, or otherwise as they direct during their lives. After the death of both grantors the successor trustee shall distribute the trust estate to the following beneficiary or beneficiaries who shall survive both grantors: _____*(names and addresses)*_____

_____

_____ .

The share of any beneficiary who shall be under the age of _____*(age)*_____ years shall not be paid to such beneficiary but shall instead be held in trust to apply to his/her use all the income thereof, and also such amounts of the principal, even to the extent of all, as the trustees deem necessary or suitable for the support, welfare and education of such beneficiary; and when he/she attains the age of _____*(age)*_____ years, to pay him/her the remaining principal, if any. If any beneficiary for whom a share is held in trust should die before having received all the principal thereof, then upon his/her death the remaining principal shall be paid to his/her then living child or children, equally if more than one, and in default thereof, to the then living descendants of the grantors, per stirpes. No interest hereunder shall be transferrable or assignable by any beneficiary, or be subject during his or her life to the claims of his or her creditors. Notwithstanding anything herein to the contrary, the trusts hereunder shall terminate not later than twenty-one (21) years after the death of the last beneficiary named herein.

3. *Revocation and Amendment:* The grantors, or the survivor of them, may, by signed instrument delivered to the trustees, revoke the trusts hereunder, in whole or in part, or amend this Agreement from time to time in any manner.

4. *Successor Trustees:* In the event of the death or incapacity of both co-trustees, we hereby nominate and appoint as successor trustee _____*(name and address)*_____. In the event the successor trustee does not serve we appoint whomever shall at the time be the first designated beneficiary hereunder. The trustees and their successors shall serve without bond.

5. *Trustees' Acceptance:* This trust has been accepted by trustees and will be administered in the State of _(state)_ and its validity, construction, and all rights thereunder shall be governed by the laws of that state.

In Witness Whereof, grantors and trustees have executed this Agreement on the date above written.

(Signature) _____   *(Signature)* _____
Grantor   Co-Trustee

(Signature) _____   *(Signature)* _____
Grantor   Co-Trustee

(Signature) _____
Witness (1)

(Signature) _____
Witness (2)

Sworn to and subscribed before me this _____ day of _____, 19 ____.

My Commission Expires: *(Signature)* _____
_____   Notary Public
        (date)

Exhibit A

(listing of property included in this agreement)

_____
_____
_____
_____

Form 17: Revocable Living Trust Agreement: Grantor, as Trustee, For Lifetime Use of Grantor, Then to Others

REVOCABLE LIVING TRUST AGREEMENT

This Revocable Living Trust Agreement is made this ___*(day)*___ day of ___*(month)*___, 19 ___*(year)*___, between ___*(name)*___ of ___*(address)*___, City of ___*(city)*___, State of ___*(state)*___, herein referred to as grantor, and ___*(name)*___, of ___*(address)*___, City of ___*(city)*___, State of ___*(state)*___, herein referred to as Trustee.

Whereas, grantor is now the owner of the property described in Exhibit A attached hereto and made a part hereof, and

Whereas, grantor desires to make provision for the care and management of such property, and collection of the income therefrom, and the disposition of both such income and such property in the manner herein provided:

Now, therefore, for the reasons set forth above, and in consideration of the mutual covenants set forth herein, grantor and trustee agree as follows:

1. *Transfer of Property:* Grantor, in consideration of the acceptance by trustee of the trust herein created, hereby conveys, transfers, assigns, and delivers to trustee, his/her successors in trust and assigns, the property described in Exhibit A attached hereto and made a part hereof, by this reference, which property, together with all other property that may from time to time be held by trustee hereunder, is herein referred to as Trust Estate. Grantor, and any other persons shall have the right at any time to add property acceptable to trustee to this trust and such property, when received and accepted by trustee, shall become a part of the trust estate.

2. *Disposition of Income and Principal:* Trustee shall care for and manage the trust estate and collect the income derived therefrom, and, after the payment of all taxes and assessments thereon and all charges incident to the management thereof, dispose of the net income therefrom and corpus thereof, as follows:

During the lifetime of grantor the trustee may pay income of the trust estate and such portions of the principal as the grantor from time to time may direct to the grantor, or otherwise as he/she may direct during his/her life. After the death of the grantor the trustee or successor trustee shall distribute the trust estate to the following beneficiary or beneficiaries who shall survive the grantor: ___*(names and addresses)*___

_____

_____ .

The share of any beneficiary who shall be under the age of ___*(age)*___ years shall not be paid to such beneficiary but shall instead be held in trust to apply to his/her use all the income thereof, and also such amounts of the principal, even to the extent of all, as the trustee deems necessary or suitable for the support, welfare and education of such beneficiary; and when he/she attains the age of ___*(age)*___ years, to pay him/her the remaining principal, if any. If any beneficiary for whom a share is held in trust should die before having received all the principal thereof, then upon his/her death the remaining principal shall be paid to his/her then living child or children, equally if more than one, and in default thereof, to the then living descendants of the grantor, per stirpes. No interest hereunder shall be transferrable or assignable by any beneficiary, or be subject during his or her life to the claims of his or her creditors. Notwithstanding anything herein to the contrary, the trusts hereunder shall terminate not later than twenty-one years after the death of the last beneficiary named herein.

3. *Revocation and Amendment:* The grantor may, by signed instrument delivered to the trustee, revoke the trusts hereunder, in whole or in part, or amend this Agreement from time to time in any manner.

4. *Successor Trustees:* In the event of the death or incapacity of any trustee, I hereby nominate and appoint as successor trustee ___*(name and address)*___. In the event the successor trustee does not serve I appoint whomever shall at the time be the first designated beneficiary hereunder. The trustees and their successors shall serve without bond.

5. *Trustee Acceptance:* This trust has been accepted by trustee and will be administered in the State of *(state)* and its validity, construction, and all rights thereunder shall be governed by the laws of that state.

In Witness Whereof, grantors and trustees have executed this Agreement on the date above written.

(Signature) _____   *(Signature)* _____
Grantor   Co-Trustee

(Signature) _____
Grantor

(Signature) _____
Witness (1)

(Signature) _____
Witness (2)

Sworn to and subscribed before me this _____ day of _____, 19 ____.

My Commission Expires: *(Signature)* _____
_____   Notary Public
      (date)

Exhibit A

_____ *(listing of property included in this agreement)* _____
_____
_____
_____
_____

Form 18: Revocable Living Trust Agreement: Grantor and Third Party, as Co-Trustees, For Lifetime Use of Grantor, Then to Others

REVOCABLE LIVING TRUST AGREEMENT

This Revocable Living Trust Agreement is made this ___*(day)*___ day of ___*(month)*___, 19 ___*(year)*___, between ___*(name)*___ of ___*(address)*___, City of ___*(city)*___, State of ___*(state)*___, herein referred to as grantor, and ___*(name)*___ and _____*(name)*_____, herein referred to as co-trustees.

Whereas, grantor is now the owner of the property described in Exhibit A attached hereto and made a part hereof, and

Whereas, grantor desires to make provision for the care and management of such property, the collection of the income therefrom, and the disposition of both such income and such property in the manner herein provided:

Now, therefore, for the reasons set forth above, and in consideration of the mutual covenants set forth herein, grantor and trustees agree as follows:

1. *Transfer of Property:* Grantor, in consideration of the acceptance by trustee of the trust herein created, hereby conveys, transfers, assigns, and delivers to trustees, their successors in trust and assigns, the property described in Exhibit A attached hereto and made a part hereof, by this reference, which property, together with all other property that may from time to time be held by trustees hereunder, is herein referred to as Trust Estate. Grantor, and any other persons shall have the right at any time to add property acceptable to trustees to this trust and such property, when received and accepted by trustees, shall become a part of the trust estate.

2. *Disposition of Income and Principal:* Trustees shall care for and manage the trust estate and collect the income derived therefrom, and, after the payment of all taxes and assessments thereon and all charges incident to the management thereof, dispose of the net income therefrom and corpus thereof, as follows:

During the lifetime of grantor the trustees may pay income of the trust estate and such portions of the principal as the grantor from time to time may direct to the grantor, or otherwise as he/she directs during his or her lifetime. After the death of grantor the successor trustee shall distribute the trust estate to the following beneficiary or beneficiaries who shall survive me: _____ *(names and addresses)*_____

_____

_____.

The share of any beneficiary who shall be under the age of ____*(age)*____ years shall not be paid to such beneficiary but shall instead be held in trust to apply to his/her use all the income thereof, and also such amounts of the principal, even to the extent of all, as the trustee deems necessary or suitable for the support, welfare and education of such beneficiary; and when he/she attains the age of ____*(age)*____ years, to pay him/her the remaining principal, if any. If any beneficiary for whom a share is held in trust should die before having received all the principal thereof, then upon his/her death the remaining principal shall be paid to his/her then living child or children, equally if more than one, and in default thereof, to the then living descendants of the grantor, per stirpes. No interest hereunder shall be transferrable or assignable by any beneficiary, or be subject during his or her life to the claims of his or her creditors. Notwithstanding anything herein to the contrary, the trusts hereunder shall terminate not later than twenty-one (21) years after the death of the last beneficiary named herein.

3. *Revocation and Amendment:* The grantor may, by signed instrument delivered to the trustee, revoke the trusts hereunder, in whole or in part, or amend this Agreement from time to time in any manner.

4. *Successor Trustees:* In the event of the death or incapacity of both trustees, I hereby nominate and appoint as successor trustee __*(name and address)*__. In the event the successor trustee does not serve I appoint whomever shall at the time be the first designated beneficiary hereunder. The trustees and their successors shall serve without bond.

5. *Trustees' Acceptance:* This trust has been accepted by trustees and will be administered in the State of _(state)_ and its validity, construction, and all rights thereunder shall be governed by the laws of that state.

In Witness Whereof, grantors and trustees have executed this Agreement on the date above written.

(Signature)	*(Signature)*
Grantor	Co-Trustee
(Signature)	*(Signature)*
Witness (1)	Co-Trustee
(Signature)	
Witness (2)	

Sworn to and subscribed before me this _____ day of _____, 19 ____.

My Commission Expires: *(Signature)*
_____*(date)*_____   Notary Public

Exhibit A

_____ *(listing of property included in this agreement)* _____

_____

_____
_____
_____

Form 19: Revocable Living Trust Agreement: Grantor to Third Party, as Trustee, For Lifetime Use of Grantor, Then to Others

REVOCABLE LIVING TRUST AGREEMENT

This Revocable Living Trust Agreement is made this ____*(day)*____ day of ____*(month)*____, 19 ___*(year)*___, between ___*(name)*___ of ___*(address)*___, City of ____*(city)*____, State of ___*(state)*___, herein referred to as Grantor, and ___*(name)*___, of ___*(address)*___, City of ____*(city)*____, State of ___*(state)*___, herein referred to as Trustee.

Whereas, grantor is now the owner of the property described in Exhibit A attached hereto and made a part hereof, and

Whereas, grantor desires to make provision for the care and management of such property, the collection of the income therefrom, and the disposition of both such income and such property in the manner herein provided:

Now, therefore, for the reasons set forth above, and in consideration of the mutual covenants set forth herein, grantor and trustee agree as follows:

1. *Transfer of Property:* Grantor, in consideration of the acceptance by trustee of the trust herein created, hereby conveys, transfers, assigns, and delivers to trustee, his/her successors in trust and assigns, the property described in Exhibit A attached hereto and made a part hereof, by this reference, which property, together with all other property that may from time to time be held by trustee hereunder, is herein referred to as Trust Estate. Grantor, and any other persons shall have the right at any time to add property acceptable to trustee to this trust and such property, when received and accepted by trustee, shall become a part of the trust estate.

2. *Disposition of Income and Principal:* Trustee shall care for and manage the trust estate and collect the income derived therefrom, and, after the payment of all taxes and assessments thereon and all charges incident to the management thereof, dispose of the net income therefrom and corpus thereof, as follows:

During the lifetime of grantor the trustee may pay income of the trust estate and such portions of the principal as the grantor from time to time may direct to the grantor or otherwise as he/she directs during his/her lifetime. After the death of the grantor the successor trustee shall distribute the trust estate to the following beneficiary or beneficiaries who shall survive me: _____ *(names and addresses)* _____

_____

_____ .

The share of any beneficiary who shall be under the age of ____*(age)*____ years shall not be paid to such beneficiary but shall instead be held in trust to apply to his/her use all the income thereof, and also such amounts of the principal, even to the extent of all, as the trustee deems necessary or suitable for the support, welfare and education of such beneficiary; and when he/she attains the age of ____*(age)*____ years, to pay him/her the remaining principal, if any. If any beneficiary for whom a share is held in trust should die before having received all the principal thereof, then upon his/her death the remaining principal shall be paid to his/her then living child or children, equally if more than one, and in default thereof, to the then living descendants of the grantor, per stirpes. No interest hereunder shall be transferrable or assignable by any beneficiary, or be subject during his or her life to the claims of his or her creditors. Notwithstanding anything herein to the contrary, the trusts hereunder shall terminate not later than twenty-one (21) years after the death of the last beneficiary named herein.

3. *Revocation and Amendment:* The grantor may, by signed instrument delivered to the trustee, revoke the trusts hereunder, in whole or in part, or amend this Agreement from time to time in any manner.

4. *Successor Trustee:* In the event of the death or incapacity of the trustee, I hereby nominate and appoint as successor trustee __*(name and address)*__. In the event the successor trustee does not serve I appoint whomever shall at the time be the first designated beneficiary hereunder. The trustee and his/her successors shall serve without bond.

5. *Trustee Acceptance:* This trust has been accepted by trustee and will be administered in the State of __(state)__ and its validity, construction, and all rights thereunder shall be governed by the laws of that state.

In Witness Whereof, grantor and trustee have executed this Agreement on the date above written.

(Signature) _____   *(Signature)* _____
Grantor   Trustee

(Signature) _____
Witness (1)

(Signature) _____
Witness (2)

Sworn to and subscribed before me this _____ day of _____, 19 ____.

My Commission Expires: *(Signature)* _____
        (date)   Notary Public
_____

Exhibit A

__*(listing of property included in this agreement)*__
_____
_____
_____
_____

Form 20: Revocation of Revocable Living Trust Agreement

Revocation of Revocable Living Trust Agreement

TO: _____ , Trustee
               (name)
               (address)
             (city and state)

I, ___*(name)*___, of ___*(address)*___, City of ___*(city)*___,
State of ___*(state)*___, as grantor in a Revocable Living Trust
Agreement dated ___*(date)*___, wherein you are designated
as trustee, do hereby revoke the powers and trusts created
and conferred by grantor in that Revocable Living Trust
Agreement, pursuant to the terms thereof.

I hereby direct you, as trustee, to turn over and deliver to
me all property held by you subject to the terms and provisions of the Revocable Living Trust Agreement, together with
all accumulations of interest and income.

In Witness Whereof, I have executed this instrument on the
_____ day of _____, 19 ____, at ___*(city, state)*___.

In the presence of:

*(Signature)*_____   *(Signature)*_____
Witness (1)   Grantor

*(Signature)*_____
Witness (2)

Sworn to and subscribed before me this _____ day of
_____, 19 ____.

My Commission Expires: *(Signature)*_____
           (date)   Notary Public

Other Methods of Avoiding Probate

Although the Revocable Living Trust is the classic method for avoiding probate, there are a number of other methods that you can use in your estate planning. All of them are easy to use. These plans have sometimes been referred to as *substitute wills*, in the sense that an owner of property is able to transfer it to others without having it go through the probate system by a will or statute. The use of the term *substitute will* is not literally correct, however, because probate is avoided only with respect to the specific property that is included in a probate avoidance plan; all other assets owned by a decedent would be subject to probate. Most people need a will in addition to probate avoidance plans as one does not generally wish to have all their property in a trust or other probate avoidance program. This is not to suggest that one cannot avoid probate with everything they own, but there are some general guidelines to be followed in determining who should avoid probate and for what property.

Who should avoid probate with respect to what property depends upon the particular facts and circumstances of each case. In general it is recommended that persons who are settled in their estate, family and financial affairs should implement probate avoidance plans. Settled in their affairs is an expression that refers generally to people who own capital assets that can easily be held in trust or other probate avoidance plans; whose children are no longer minors; who have reached middle age; who have substantial assets; or who simply want to save 10% to 20% or more of an estate for their

family rather than permitting it to be churned through the
probate processes.

Probate avoidance is accomplished by placing title to property in such a way that upon the death of the owner it legally
passes to another who holds it outside the jurisdiction of the
probate courts. In addition to the Revocable Living Trust this
can be accomplished by Joint Ownership, Joint Tenancy with
right of survivorship, Gifts, Life Insurance (payable to
beneficiaries other than the insured or the insured's estate),
The Irrevocable Living Trust, and The Private Annuity.

Joint Ownership

The joint ownership of property with right of survivorship
is one of the easiest ways to avoid probate. The jointly owned
property automatically becomes that of the survivor or survivors as a matter of law and no probate is needed. The joint
ownership method can be effective with real estate as well
as other property such as bank accounts, mutual funds, stocks,
bonds, automobiles, antiques, and other property. It is important for you to comply with any title certificate or recording
requirements of your state. For example, automobile certificate registration or real estate conveyances must be recorded
in both names as joint tenants.

Although every state authorizes joint ownership with right
of survivorship, the terminology may differ from state to state.
Therefore, you should use printed real estate forms designed
for your state to convey real property titles.

In most states this method of title ownership is called *Joint
Tenancy, with right of survivorship*. A few states call it an
Estate by the Entirety when used as between husband and
wife. In the eight states having Community Property laws,
property held by husband and wife is governed by the Community Property principles.

Joint Tenancy, With Right Of Survivorship (JTWROS)

An estate in joint tenancy is one held by two or more persons jointly, with equal rights to share in its enjoyment during their lives, and having as its distinguishing feature the right of survivorship, or *jus accrescendi*, by virtue of which the entire estate, upon the death of a joint tenant, goes to the survivor or, in the case of more than two joint tenants, to the survivors, and so on to the last survivor, free and exempt from all charges made by the deceased co-tenant or co-tenants.

One of the great advantages of the doctrine of survivorship is that a joint tenant cannot devise interest in the land, for the devise does not take effect until after the death of the decedent, and the claim of the surviving tenant arises in the same instant with that of the devisee and is preferred thereto. It is equally clear that the interests of the deceased tenant cannot descend to his heirs or pass to his representatives under the laws regulating intestate succession. A surviving joint tenant holds under the conveyance or instrument by which the tenancy was created and not under laws regulating intestate succession. Furthermore, the creditors of a deceased joint tenant do not have any recourse against the surviving joint tenant who requires the property under such instrument.

At common law and also under the law as it generally prevails at present, the creation and the continued existence of a joint tenancy depends upon the coexistence of four requisites.

- The tenants must have one and the same interest.
- The interests must accrue by one and the same conveyance.
- They must commence at one and the same time.
- The property must be held by one and the same undivided possession.

In other words, there must be the following four unities: unity of interest, unity of title, unity of time, and unity of possession. If any one of these elements is lacking, the estate will not be one in joint tenancy.

In most states, these principles have been codified and are regulated by statute. When in doubts, consult the specific statutes of your own state. All natural persons can be seized or possessed of such an estate, and in most states other entities can be joint tenants.

Although most people think of joint tenancy as confined to interests in real property, it is settled that a joint tenancy of such character can exist in any kind of property. Joint ownership of bank accounts, savings accounts, brokerage accounts, and other such titles are regulated by statutes in most states, and this can easily be determined from your financial institutions. It is recommended that you discuss the subject with any financial institution where you do business to make certain that they understand, and comply with, your desires and instructions. You can't depend upon a bank, insurance company, or other financial institution to arbitrarily do your estate planning by blindly following some inter-office memo or procedure manual. They must be directed to record your accounts exactly as you specify.

You should not confuse a joint tenancy, with right of survivorship (JTWROS), with a tenancy in common. They are, legally, very different. Tenancy in common is a tenancy whereby two or more persons are entitled to land in such manner that they have an undivided possession, but several freeholds or interests. In a tenancy in common, which is not limited to husband and wife, there is no right of survivorship. Each owns undivided interests in the property. Either co-owner may dispose of his or her undivided interest in the property during his or her life, or by will. When one co-owner dies, his or her interest (an undivided interest) does not go to the surviving co-owner, but to the decedent's heirs or according to will. Therefore, this kind of ownership does not avoid probate.

Tenancy by the Entirety

A tenancy by the entirety or *Estate by the Entirety*, exists only where the co-owners are husband and wife. When either spouse dies, the survivor becomes the sole owner by right of survivorship. The right of survivorship cannot be destroyed during the lives of the co-owners except with the consent of both. In some states, this form of ownership exists only with respect to real property. In a few states it may exist in the case of personal property. For historical reasons the term Estate by the Entirety is still used in some states, but the legal effect is the same as the Joint Tenancy, with right of survivorship (JTWROS).

Community Property

Community Property is property owned in common by husband and wife, each having an undivided one-half interest by reason of their marital status. The eight states with community property laws are Arizona, California, Idaho, Louisiana, Nevada, New Mexico and Washington. The other states are governed by common law principles. Community Property is that property that remains after family living expenses and all other community debts have been paid. It is said to be a fundamental postulate of the community property system that whatever is gained during coventure, by the toil, talent, or other productive faculty of either spouse, is community property. Community Property, under the statutes, usually includes all property acquired by either spouse during a marriage, other than by gift, devise, or descent.

Community Property is not known to the common law or to Roman law. In the United States, Community Property derives its existence from express legislation. It is a creature of statute and can exist only under the circumstances expressly provided for. The disposition of the property upon the death of husband or wife is governed by the statutes.

Gifts

Property which you give away is no longer a part of your estate for probate purposes. Therefore you avoid probate with respect to that property. Gift taxes can be assessed, but there is an unlimited exemption for spouses, and a $10,000 exclusion annually per donee. Therefore, gifts can be used as an estate planning tool for avoiding probate and, with proper planning, for avoiding both gift and estate taxes.

Life Insurance

Generally, life insurance is payable directly to the designated beneficiaries and is not a part of an estate for probate purposes. Moreover, you can avoid estate taxes on insurance if you and your estate do not retain any ownership or interest in the insurance contract. Typically, you can have your spouse or other family member own life insurance policies on your life, and it does not become a part of your estate for probate purposes, or for tax purposes.

Irrevocable Living Trust

An irrevocable living trust, as its name indicates, is one that cannot be revoked or changed. It is final. There are some tax advantages in using an irrevocable trust, and it also has most of the advantages of a revocable trust. This trust can be used for gifts, typically to minors. The assets in an irrevocable trust will avoid the probate system, avoid estate taxes in some circumstances, avoid income taxes to the grantor, and the trustee can manage the property for the beneficiaries if needed.

FORM 21: Irrevocable Trust Agreement

TRUST AGREEMENT

This Irrevocable Trust Agreement is made this _(day)_ day of _(month)_, 19 _(year)_, between _(name)_ of _(address)_, City of _(city)_, County of _(county)_, State of _(state)_, herein referred to as Grantor, and _(name)_ of _(address)_, City of _(city)_, County of _(county)_, State of _(state)_, herein referred to as Trustee.

In consideration of the mutual covenants and promises set forth herein, Grantor and Trustee agree as follows:

1. Transfer of Trust. Grantor herewith assigns, transfers, and conveys to Trustee the property described in Exhibit "A," attached hereto and made a part hereof by this reference, and receipt of such property is hereby acknowledged by Trustee. Such property, hereafter designated the Trust Estate, shall be held by Trustee in Trust for the uses and purposes and on the terms and conditions set forth herein.

2. Disposition of Principal and Income. Trustee shall administer and manage the Trust Estate, collect the income therefrom, and, after payment of all taxes and assessments thereon and all charges incident to the management thereof, apply and dispose of the net income and the principal of the Trust Estate as follows: _(names and addresses of beneficiaries)_

_____

_____.

3. Additions to Trust. Grantor and any other person shall have the right at any time to add property acceptable to Trustee to this Trust. Such property, when received and accepted by Trustee, shall become part of the Trust Estate.

4. Irrevocability of Trust. This trust shall be irrevocable and shall not be revoked or terminated by Grantor or any other person, nor shall it be amended or altered by Grantor or any other person.

5. Compensation of Trustee: The original Trustee hereunder, and all Successor Trustees, shall be entitled to reasonable compensation for their services as Trustee.

6. Successor Trustees. If ___*(name)*___ (Original Trustee) resigns or is unable to continue to act as Trustee, *(name)* (Successor Trustee), of ___*(address)*___, City of ___*(city)*___, County of ___*(county)*___, State of ___*(state)*___, is hereby appointed as Successor Trustee.

7. Governing Laws. The validity, construction, and effect of this agreement and of the Trust created hereunder and its enforcement shall be determined by the laws of the State of ___*(state)*___.

In Witness Whereof, Grantor and Trustee have executed this agreement on the date above written.

*(Signature)*_____   *(Signature)*_____
Grantor   Trustee

*(Signature)*_____   *(Signature)*_____
Witness (1)   Successor Trustee

*(Signature)*_____
Witness (2)

STATE OF _____
COUNTY OF _____ ss

The foregoing instrument was acknowledged before me this _____ day of _____, 19 ___, by *(name)* (Grantor), ___*(name)*___ (Trustee), and ___*(name)*___, Successor Trustee.

                                       *(Signature)*_____
                                       Notary Public
My Commission Expires:
_____
     (date)

EXHIBIT "A"
___*(listing of property included in this agreement)*___
_____
_____
_____

Private Annuity

The private annuity, a relatively unpublicized estate planning technique, is another easy plan for avoiding probate. Moreover, it is a superior estate tax avoidance plan when used in the right circumstances. This plan can be utilized both to avoid estate taxes and to avoid probate. The private annuity is an agreement where an estate owner transfers property to another person, whose business is not selling annuities, in exchange for an unsecured promise to pay for the property in periodic payments for the remainder of the owner's life. Typically, the agreement is between family members or between a shareholder and a closely held corporation.

For the older estate owner the private annuity offers several distinct advantages in addition to avoidance of probate. It provides the taxpayer with a means of passing property to the persons he wishes to have it. It decreases his taxable estate. It affords an opportunity to transfer a going business to those who are capable of managing it. The owner is assured of income for the remainder of his life.

There are two types of private annuities: the single life annuity under which payments cease at the death of the owner, and the joint and last survivor annuity, in which payments continue until the death of the last survivor. For example, in the latter, payments continue as long as either the husband or wife is alive. Since payments under this type of arrangement will continue for longer than payments under a single life annuity, the amounts paid each year will be less than that payable under a single life annuity.

A private annuity should be considered for use under the following circumstances:
- You wish to avoid probate.
- You have a need to spread capital gains.
- You wish to retire and shift control of a business to a family member or to a key employee.
- You desire to remove a sizable asset from your estate for estate tax purposes.
- You wish to obtain a fixed retirement income.

- You own a large parcel of non-income producing property but want to make it income producing.
- Other situations where you wish to convey property to others with long term payments.

There are certain requirements under the Internal Revenue Code for setting up a private annuity to effectively avoid estate taxes. Although any type of property can be used, income producing property is the most appropriate. For the plan to be successul it is necessary for the transferee to be in a financial condition to make payments during the period of the annuity. If the transferee has substantial independent income, then almost any asset can serve as the property to be transferred. However, if the transferee does not have sufficient income or resources to make the payments then the property sold should be either income producing or at least should be of a type that the transferee can use it to generate income.

This is important because the transferee's promise to make the payments must be unsecured. If the promise of the transferee is secured a taxable event will occur immediately upon the transfer, and the transferor would be required to pay taxes on the full amount of the gain, if any. Of course, even if tax advantages are not the major reason for this annuity, it still avoids probate.

The transferee should be a person not regularly engaged in issuing private annuities. The transferee is usually a family member, key employee, or other persons who are close to the owner. For example, most private annuities are made between parents and children. The annuity amount must be determined by measuring the value and cost basis of the property. In other words, it must be a sale and not a gift.

The procedure for arranging a private annuity is quite simple. Draw up a written agreement for the sale of property in return for the payment by the transferee. The payments must be based upon actuarial tables and relate to the age of the transferor or other recipient of the payments. Use form 22 as an example of the private annuity agreement.

Form 22: The Private Annuity Agreement

PRIVATE ANNUITY AGREEMENT

This annuity Agreement is made this _____*(day)*_____ day of _*(month)*_, 19 _*(year)*_, by and between _*(name)*_, of _*(city, state)*_ hereinafter called Transferor, and her son, _____*(name)*_____, also of ___*(city, state)*___, hereinafter called the Transferee.

Whereas, Transferor is the owner of that certain real estate situate, lying and being in _____*(county)*_____ County, State of _____*(state)*_____, and more particularly described as: *(address as on deed)* *(Legal Description)*.

Whereas, Transferor is _*(age)*_ years of age and wishes to be free of the liabilities of the management of real property and wishes to be assured of a fixed annual income for the remainder of her life, regardless of whether such property is rented; and

Whereas, the market value of said property is $ _____ according to an appraisal made by _____*(name)*_____, and Transferor's basis in said property is $_____; and

Whereas, Transferee wishes to acquire said property as an investment and is willing to make fixed annual payments of $_____ for the remainder of Transferor's life in exchange for said property.

Now, Therefore, for and in consideration of the mutual promises made by each party to the other and of the mutual agreement contained herein, the parties hereto agree with each other as follows:

1. The Transferor shall this day execute and deliver to the Transferee a good and sufficient Warranty Deed conveying all of her right, title, and interest in and to the above described real property. Transferor shall pay all costs in connection with the preparation of the Deed and any transfer taxes due.

2. Transferee, for himself, his heirs, and legal representatives does hereby agree to pay to the Transferor the sum of $_____ for her lifetime, payable on the *(number)* day of *(each month, quarter, year, etc.)*, the first payment to be made on _____*(date)*_____.

3. The parties agree that taxes, insurance, and rentals shall be prorated as of the _(day)_ day of _(month)_, 19_(year)_. Transferee shall pay all expenses in connection with the title examination and survey he has caused to be made in connection with his acquisition of said property. He shall also pay all recording fees.

4. The aforesaid payments to the Transferor are to be made without reference to the transferred property and irrespective of any income earned by the property. These payments are obligations of the Transferee and are not limited in any way to the value of the property.

5. The Transferee is given the right to sell, transfer, assign, or pledge the property free and clear of any claims whatsoever by the Transferor and it is understood that the payments to be made to the Transferor are not secured by the property.

6. This agreement shall inure to the benefit of and shall be binding upon the Transferee's heirs and legal representatives.

In Witness Whereof, this Annuity Agreement is signed, sealed, and delivered in duplicate on the day and year first written above.

(Signature) _____   _(Signature)_ _____
Transferor   Transferee

Glossary of Legal Terms

Abatement: A proportional reduction of a debt or legacy due, where the fund or the estate is insufficient to meet full payment.

Acknowledgment: Formal declaration before an authorized official, by the person who executed the instrument, that it is his free act and deed.

Ademption: The extinction or satisfaction of a legacy by some act of the testator, which indicates either a revocation of, or an intention to, revoke the bequest.

Administration of Estates: Supervision by an executor or administrator. Management of the estate by an independent executor. Normally involves the collection, management, and distribution of an estate, including the legal proceedings necessary to satisfy claims of creditors, next of kin, legatees, or other parties who may have any claim to the property of a deceased person.

Administrator/Administratrix: In probate practice, a person to whom letters of administration, that is, an authority to administer the estate of a deceased person, have been granted by the proper court. An administrator resembles an executor, but, being appointed by the court, and not by the deceased, he has to give security for the due administration of the estate, by entering into a bond with sureties, called an administration bond. Administrator refers to a male and administratrix to a female.

Advancement: An irrevocable gift made *inter vivos* (during lifetime) by a parent to a child, with the intent that the gift is to represent all or part of the parent's estate to which the child would be entitled on the death of the parent intestate (dying without a will). An advancement is distinguished from a debt or loan in that an advancement involves a transfer of property without consideration and is also distinguished from a gift in that while the advancement need not be repaid it requires the donee to account for the gift before he or she is permitted to share in the intestate's estate.

Affinity: Relation which one spouse, because of marriage, has to blood relatives of the other; consanguinity is relation by blood.

Ancestor: One from whom a person lineally descended or may be descended; a progenitor.

Ancillary Administration: Administration in a state where decedent has property and which is other than where decedent was domiciled.

Antenuptial: A contract made before marriage between the parties as to their property rights.

Appraisal: A valuation or an estimation of value of property, usually by two disinterested persons of suitable qualifications.

Attestation: The act of witnessing an instrument in writing at the request of the party making it, and subscribing it as a witness.

Beneficiary: One for whose benefit a trust is created; a person having the enjoyment of property of which a trustee, executor, administrator or other has the legal possession; a person to whom a policy of insurance is payable.

Bequest: A gift of personal property.

Codicil: Addition to or qualification of one's last will and testament.

Collateral Descent: In intestacy, this refers to descent of the intestate's heirs who are neither his descendants nor his ancestors but are those who at some point share a common ancestor with the intestate. These heirs are the intestate's collaterals. Brother or sister, uncle or aunt, nephew or niece, and so on, are all in this category.

Common Law: The general and ordinary law of a community receiving its binding force from universal reception. Historically, that body of law and juristic theory which was originated, developed, and formulated in England.

Community Property: The property acquired by either spouse during marriage, other than by gift, devise, or descent based on the doctrine that property acquired during marriage belongs to the marital community. Community property states are Arizona, California, Idaho, Louisiana, Nevada, New Mexico, Texas and Washington.

Competent Witness: A person who, at the time of attesting to a will, could legally testify in court to the facts to which he attests by subscribing his name to the will.

Conditional Will: A will that becomes effective upon the happening of a specified condition or contingency.

Consanguinity: Blood relationship; kinship; the connection or relation of persons descended from the same stock or common ancestor.

Conservator: A guardian, protector, preserver. Generally appointed by a court to care for the property of another.

Constructive Trust: A trust by operation of law, as distinguished from an expressed trust. By construction of law, a court will establish a constructive trust in favor of one party and against another, when title is actually in the name of the latter, but when by either mistake or fraud the former has been deprived of what is rightfully his.

Contemplation of Death: An apprehension or expectation of approaching dissolution; not that general expectation which every mortal entertains, but the apprehension which arises from some presently existing sickness or physical condition or from some impending danger. As applied to transfers of property, the phrase *in contemplation of death* means that thought of death is the impelling cause of transfer and that motive which induces transfer is of the sort which leads to testamentary disposition and is practically equivalent to *causa mortis.* The Internal Revenue Code contains a statutory definition of the term which must be applied for tax purposes.

Curtesy: Under the common law rules a husband had a right in any real property of which his wife was seized at any time during the marriage. The husband's right, termed "curtesy" was inchoate during his wife's lifetime and consummate after her death if he survived her and if a child was born of the marriage. Curtesy entitled the husband to a life estate in all of the wife's free-hold property owned by her during the marriage. It could not be defeated or by her *inter vivos* transfer or by the wife's will, and it was not subject to her debts.

Decease: To die; to depart life, or from life.

Decedent: A deceased person, especially one who has recently died.

Descendant: One who is descended from another; a person who proceeds from the body of another, such as child, grandchild, to the remotest degree.

Descent: Historically the intestate decedent's real property passed directly to his heirs by operation of law. Thus, real property was said to pass by *descent* to the heirs who took by inheritance.

Devise: A gift of real property by will; a *devisor devises* real property to a *devisee* and the disposition is termed a *devise.*

Disposing Memory: One in which a person can recall the general nature, condition, and extent of property and his relations to those to whom he gives and to those from whom he withholds that property.

Distribution: Historically this meant title to the intestate decedent's personal propety vested in his personal representative who subsequently *distributed* it to the intestate's distributees or next of kin, after the administration of the estate which was the collection and preservation of the decedent's personal property, and the payment of his creditors.

Domicile: That place where a person has his/her true fixed and permanent home and principal establishment, and to which whenever he is absent he has the intention of returning.

Dower: Under the common law rules a wife had a right in any real property of which her husband was seized at any time during the marriage. The wife's right termed *dower* was inchoate during her husband's lifetime and consummate after his death if she survived him. The dower interest was a life estate in one-third of the real property of which the husband had been seized during the marriage. Dower could not be defeated by transfer by the husband during his lifetime or by his will, and the wife's interest was not subject to claims of his creditors. In most states this common law rule is now covered by statute and is frequently referred to as statutory share.

Escheat: In American law, a reversion of property to the state in consequence of the lack of any individual competent to inherit it.

Estate: This term refers to all the property owned by a decedent at his death and which passes either by his will or by the laws of intestacy. The estate for death tax purposes is not necessarily the same as for administration purposes. The value of many assets may be subject to death taxation though the assets are not subject to administration.

Estate Taxes: Taxes assessed by states and the federal government upon the decedent's right to transfer property. A succession, legacy, or inheritance tax is a tax upon the right to receive property.

Executor/Executrix: A person appointed by a testator to carry out the directions and requests in his will, and to dispose of the property according to his testamentary provisions after his decease.

Fiduciary: The term is derived from the Roman law, and, as a noun, means a person holding the character of a trustee, or the trust and confidence involved in it and the scrupulous good faith and candor which it requires. A person having a duty to act primarily for the benefit of another in matters connected with the undertaking. It is something in the nature of a trust, having the characteristics of a trust, analogous to a trust, relating to or founded upon a trust of confidence.

Fraud: An intentional perversion of truth for the purpose of inducing another, in reliance upon it, to part with some valuable thing belonging to him or to surrender a legal right. A false representation of a matter of fact, whether by words or by conduct, by false or misleading representations, or by concealment of that which should have been disclosed, which deceives, and is intended to deceive another so that he shall act upon it to his legal detriment.

General Legacy: A legacy which is payable out of the general assets of the testator's estate, such as a gift of money, or other thing in quantity, and not in any way separated or distinguished from other things of like kind.

Gift: A voluntary transfer of personal property without consideration.

Gift Causa Mortis: A gift of personalty made in expectation of death, then imminent, on an essential condition that the property shall belong fully to the donee in case the donor dies as anticipated, leaving the donee surviving him, and the gift is not in the meantime revoked.

Gift Inter Vivos: Gifts between the living, which are prefected and become absolute during the lifetime of the donor and the donee.

Guardian: A guardian is a person lawfully invested with power, and charged with the duty, of taking care of the person and managing the property and rights of another person, who, for some peculiarity of status, or defect of age, understanding, or self-control, is considered incapable of administering his own affairs. One who legally has the care and management of the person, or the estate, or both, of a child during its minority.

Guardian Ad Litem: A person appointed by a court to look after the interests of an infant whose property is involved in litigation.

Heirs: Historically this had reference to those who took title to an intestate's real property by descent. Many state statutes now define the word to include those persons who take both real and personal property of the intestate. A living person has no heirs, but only heirs apparent.

Holographic Will: A testamentary instrument entirely written, dated, and signed by the testator in his own handwriting. In some states, by statute, based on the Uniform Probate Code, it is only required that the signature and material provisions of the will be in the testator's handwriting.

Incompetency: Lack of ability, legal qualification, or fitness to discharge the required duty.

In Extremis: An extremity; in the last extremity; in the last illness.

Inheritance Taxes: Taxes assessed on the recipient of the assets and based on the right to receive a decedent's property.

Inter Vivos: Between the living; from one living person to another; gifts during one's lifetime.

Intestacy: The state or condition of a person dying without having made a valid will, or without having disposed by will of a part of his property.

Intestate: Without making a will. A person is said to die intestate when he dies without making a will, or dies without leaving anything to testify what his wishes were with respect to the disposal of his property after his death.

Intestate Laws: Statutes which provide and prescribe the devolution of estates of persons who die without disposing of their estates by law, will or testament.

Intestate Succession: A succession is called intestate when the deceased has left no will, or when his will has been revoked or annulled as irregular. The heirs to whom a succession has fallen by the effects of law only are called *heirs ab intestato*.

Irrevocable: That which cannot be revoked or recalled.

Legacies: Gifts of property under a will.

Legatee: One who receives property under a will.

Letters: This is the name given to the document issued, under court seal, to evidence to others the appointment and authority of the personal representative.

Letters of Administration: The instrument by which an administrator or administratrix is authorized by probate court, surrogate, or other proper office, to have the charge and administration of the goods and chattels of an intestate.

Letters Testamentary: The formal instrument of authority and appointment given to an executor by the proper court, upon the admission of the will to probate, empowering him to enter upon the discharge of his office as executor.

Life Interest: Interest held only during the term of a person's life.

Lineal Descent: In intestacy this refers to descent to the intestate's heirs who are his descendants, in an indefinite line of succession. For example, child, grandchild, great-grandchild, and so on.

Litigation: Lawsuit; a contest in a court of justice for the purpose of enforcing a right.

Lunatic: A person of deranged or unsound mind, or one whose mental facilities are in the condition called *lunacy.* One who possessed reason, but through disease, grief, or other cause has lost it.

Lucid Interval: A temporary cure, a temporary restoration to sanity.

Monomania: In medical jurisprudence, derangement of a single facility of the mind, or with regard to a particular subject, the other facilities being in regular exercise.

Non Compos Mentis: A condition approximating total and positive incompetency. It denotes a person entirely destitute of memory and understanding.

Nuncupative Will: An oral declaration by the testator *in extremis,* or under circumstances considered equivalent thereto, as to the .final disposition of his property, made before witnesses, and subsequently reduced to writing by someone other than the testator. Specific requirements and limitations are set out in the statutes in the states where these wills are valid.

Obliteration: Erasure or blotting out of written words.

Paranoia: Delusional insanity or monomania.

Partial Insanity: A term applied to cases wherein the mind is clouded or weakened, but is not entirely incapable of remembering, reasoning, or judging.

Passage of Title Under A Will: Title to real property passes directly to the devisee, subject to the claims of testator's creditors, but the personal representative has the right of possession during administration. Title and possession of personal property pass to the personal representative and only upon distribution of the estate does the legatee receive title and possession.

Per Capita: Equally, or share and share alike.

Perjury: The willful assertion as to a matter of fact, opinion, belief, or knowledge, made by a witness in a judicial proceeding as part of his evidence, either upon oath or in any form allowed by law to be substituted for an oath, whether such evidence is given in open court, or in an affidavit, or otherwise, such assertion being material to the issue or point or inquiry and known to such witness to be false.

Per Stirpes (by the stalk): According to the roots, or by right of representation; the issue of deceased children will take their deceased parent's share by right of representation. That mode of reckoning the rights or liabilities of descendants in which the children of any one descendant have to take only the share which their parents would have taken, if alive. For example, suppose a decedent had three children, Jim, Jane and John, who, if living, would get one third each. If John predeceased the decedent and left ten children, the estate would be divided into twelve equal shares, if per capita. If per stirpes, the estate would be one third to Jane, one third to Jim, and the remaining one third divided among John's ten children.

Posthumous Child: A child born after the father's death.

Pretermitted Child: A child to whom a will leaves no share of the parent's estate without an affirmative provision in the will showing an intention to omit.

Probate: This word describes the presenting of a will to the appropriate court to establish its validity, and the entering of the court's order finding that the instrument is decedent's will and admitting it to probate. There follows, as in intestate estates, a process of administration, the collection and preservation of the decedent's property to those entitled to it by his will or by the statute of descent and distribution.

Probate Court: The court that has jurisdiction with respect to wills and intestacies and sometimes guardianships. Also called surrogate's court and orphan's court in some states.

Probate of Will: Formal proof before the proper officer or court that the instrument offered is the last will of the decedent.

Publication: The communication by the testator to the witnesses of his intention that the instrument in question should take effect as his will.

Remainderman: The person who receives property remaining after the death of the person who received the original life interest.

Residuary Clause: The clause in a will which specifies the disposition of all that is left after indebtedness and bequests, or gifts, are paid.

Residuary Estate: That which remains after the debts and expenses of administration, legacies, and devises have been satisfied.

Revocation of Will: The recalling, annulling or rendering inoperative of an existing will, by some subsequent act of the testator, which may be the making of a new will inconsistent with the terms of the first, or by destroying the old will, or by disposing of the property to which it related, or otherwise.

Settlor: The grantor or donor in a deed of settlement. Also one who creates a trust, or furnishes the consideration for the creation of a trust.

Specific Legacy: A gift by will of a specific article or a particular part of the testator's estate, which is identified and distinguished from all others of the same nature, and which can be satisfied only by the delivery and receipt of the particular given thing.

Spendthrift Clause: A provision in a will or trust instrument which limits the right of the beneficiary to dispose of his interest and the right of his creditors to reach it.

Spendthrift Trust: A trust which provides a fund for the benefit of a person other than the settlor, secures it against the beneficiary's own improvidence and places it beyond his creditor's reach. Provisions against alienation of the trust fund by the voluntary act of the beneficiary or by his creditors are the usual incidents of a spendthrift trust.

Statutory Share: That portion of a person's property allowed to the spouse by statute.

Subscribe: Literally to write underneath, as one's name (*sub,* under). To write below a documentary statement. In its popular meaning, it is usually limited to a signature at the end of a printed or written instrument.

Subscribing Witnesses: Those who sign as witnesses to a will.

Surrogate: In American law, the name given in some of the states to the judge or judicial officer who has the administration of probate matters, guardianships, and other such matters. In other states he is called judge of probate, registrar, judge of the orphan's court, and other titles.

Testamentary: The expression of an intent to dispose of property by will.

Testamentary Capacity: The competency to make a will.

Testamentary Guardian: A guardian named in the decedent's will.

Testamentary Power: A person who may make a will.

Testamentary Trust: A trust established by the terms of a will.

Testate: Having made and left a valid will.

Testator: A man who has left a will at his death.

Testatrix: A female who has left a will at her death.

Testimonium Clause: The execution of a will; that clause of a will or instrument which concludes, "In Witness Whereof, I ..."

Testimony: Evidence given by a competent witness, under oath or affirmation, as distinguished from evidence derived from writing and other sources.

Trust: In general, a right of property, real or personal, held by one party for the benefit of another.

Trustee: One to whom property or funds have been legally entrusted to be administered for the benefit of another; a person, usually one of the persons appointed to administer the affairs of a company, institution, or the like.

Trustor: One who creates a trust. Also called a settlor or grantor.

Valid: Sufficiently supported by actual fact, well grounded, sound, or just; good or effective, having sufficient legal strength or force; good or sufficient in point of law.

Validity: The state or quality of being valid; legal strength or force; soundness.

Void: Having no legal or binding force; null. Empty or not containing matter, vacant, unoccupied, devoid, destitute.

Will: An instrument executed by a competent person in the manner prescribed by statute, whereby he makes a disposition of his property to take effect on and after his death.

Index